W9-AVH-983

Dinosaur
LEARNING ACTIVITY
BOOK

Written and Illustrated by
Geoff Habiger

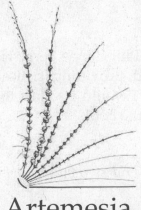

Artemesia
Publishing

Copyright © 2005 by Geoff Habiger. Printed in the United States of America.

All rights reserved, No part of this book may be reproduced or transmitted in any form or by any means, electronic or mechanical, including photocopying, recording or by any information storage or retrieval system without written permission of the publisher, except for the inclusion of brief quotations in a review. Special permission is given to educators to use the material in this book for classroom and educational purposes only.

Teachers, educators, fossil clubs, and museums: Take 40% off the cover price and use this book for fundraisers, membership drives, classroom use, or as gifts. Contact the publisher for more details.

Artemesia Publishing, LLC
P.O. Box 6508
Rocky Mount, N.C. 27802-6508
252-985-2877
info@artemesiapublishing.com
www.artemesiapublishing.com

Library of Congress Cataloging-in-Publication Data

Habiger, Geoff
    Dinosaur Learning Activity Book. / by Geoff Habiger
        p. cm.
    ISBN 1-932926-96-8
    LCCN: 2005900911

First Printing

Special thanks to Geb Bennett, Phil Currie, Jerry Harris, and Andrew Heckert for reviewing the manuscript and providing critical comments. Any errors that remain are those of the author. I would also like to thank Kenneth Carpenter and Jason Poole for their review of the book.

Cover design by Jim Gower.

Introduction:

I still have the first dinosaur book I owned. It is titled *Dinosaurs & Other Prehistoric Animals* and was written by Tom McGowen and illustrated by Rod Ruth and published in 1978. My copy is a little tattered at the edges and the spine is in need of some care, but I still enjoy looking through it. As a child I would read and reread that book hundreds of times, and from it I first learned the names of many of the most famous dinosaurs; *Tyrannosaurus*, *Triceratops*, *Stegosaurus*, and *Allosaurus*. The book was a key in developing my love and excitement for dinosaurs and other fossil animals. Eventually I went to college and got a degree in geology and started down the path to becoming a paleontologist. I've had the pleasure of digging up fossils in the badlands of Montana and molding and casting dinosaur bones. However, lives change, and my life took me away from doing paleontology in the field. I may not be digging up dinosaurs anymore, but my interest in these amazing animals has never gone away.

The Dinosaur Learning Activity Book is my way of spreading my own passion for dinosaurs to others. The book has changed many times since I first 'self-published' it at my local copy store. I am excited to have the opportunity to publish the book in an activity book format, a vision I have dreamed of since drawing the first sketches that have become the heart of this book.

The book has been updated many times since the first printing and this may not be the end of the line. The world of paleontology is dynamic and always changing, with new discoveries and updates to familiar animals made every year. I depend greatly on the skill and dedication of the paleontologists, geologists, biologists, fossil preparators, and other artists and specialists that all work together to bring dinosaurs to life. Without them this book would not be possible.

The Dinosaur Learning Activity Book was drawn and written with teachers and students in mind, but it is not limited to these groups. I have tried to keep all the material not only factual but fun too, so that anybody, young or old, will not only have fun, but also learn something about dinosaurs in the process.

I have made this book as current as possible. Any inaccuracies in the book are mine, and mine alone.

Geoff Habiger

What is a paleontologist?

A paleontologist is a person who studies "old life."

Some paleontologists study animals that lived a long time ago. Other paleontologists study plants that lived a long time ago, they are called paleobotanists.

Some paleontologists study animals that do not have a backbone. Animals without a backbone are called "invertebrates," and paleontologists that study these animals are called "invertebrate paleontologists."

Other paleontologists study animals that do have a backbone. These animals are called "vertebrates," and paleontologists that study these animals are called "vertebrate paleontologists."

Paleontologists work together with scientists like geologists, biologists, and chemists to study the history of the Earth.

Paleontologist's Tools

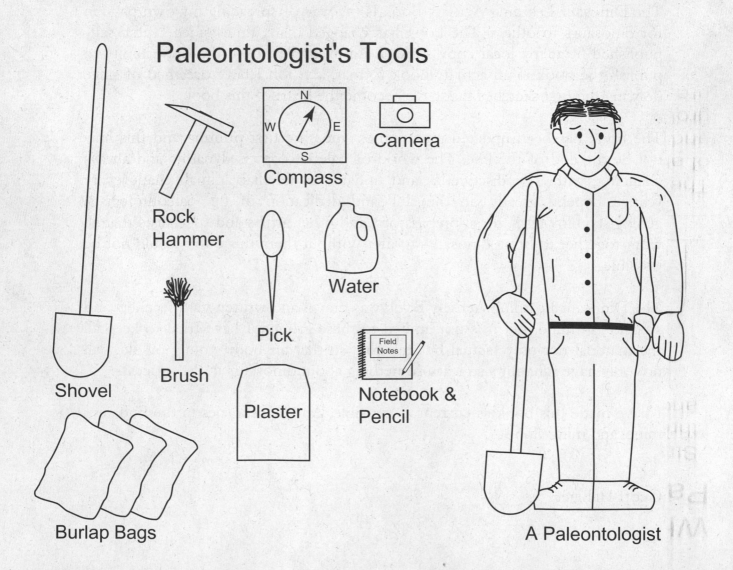

Compass

Camera

Rock Hammer

Water

Pick

Brush

Field Notes

Notebook & Pencil

Shovel

Plaster

Burlap Bags

A Paleontologist

What makes a dinosaur a dinosaur?
Part I: Stance

Stance is a description of how an animal stands. There are three basic types of stance: **sprawling**, **semi-sprawling**, and **erect**.

Sprawling Stance

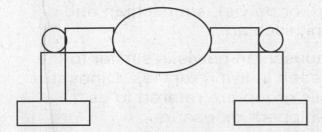

The sprawling stance is typical of animals like lizards. The thighs and upper arms are parallel to the ground and the knees and elbows are bent at right angles.

Semi-sprawling Stance

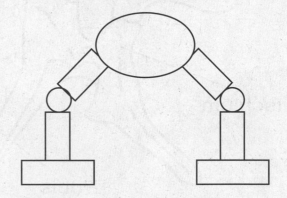

The semi-spawling stance is seen in animals like crocodiles. Here, the thighs and upper arms are turned slightly downward and the knees and elbows are only slightly bent.

Erect Stance

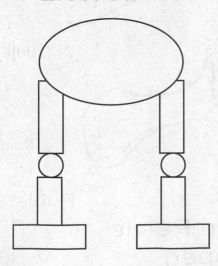

The erect stance is seen in many different animals including dinosaurs and mammals. In this stance the thighs and upper arms point straight down so the knees and elbows are straight.

What makes a dinosaur a dinosaur?
Part II: Dinosaur Hips

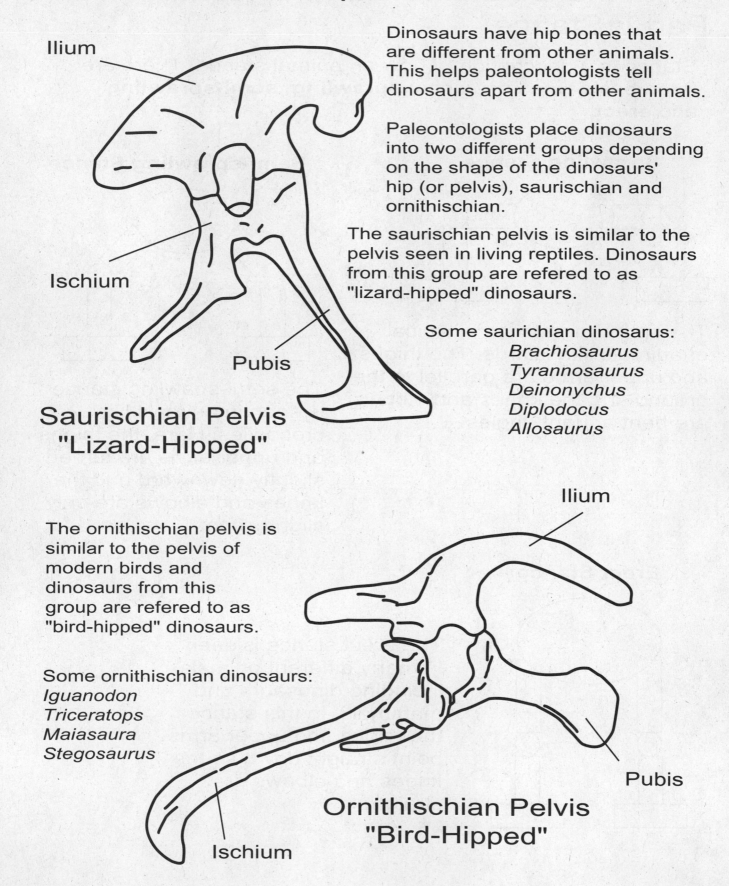

Ilium

Ischium

Pubis

Saurischian Pelvis
"Lizard-Hipped"

Dinosaurs have hip bones that are different from other animals. This helps paleontologists tell dinosaurs apart from other animals.

Paleontologists place dinosaurs into two different groups depending on the shape of the dinosaurs' hip (or pelvis), saurischian and ornithischian.

The saurischian pelvis is similar to the pelvis seen in living reptiles. Dinosaurs from this group are refered to as "lizard-hipped" dinosaurs.

Some saurichian dinosarus:
Brachiosaurus
Tyrannosaurus
Deinonychus
Diplodocus
Allosaurus

The ornithischian pelvis is similar to the pelvis of modern birds and dinosaurs from this group are refered to as "bird-hipped" dinosaurs.

Some ornithischian dinosaurs:
Iguanodon
Triceratops
Maiasaura
Stegosaurus

Ilium

Pubis

Ischium

Ornithischian Pelvis
"Bird-Hipped"

Where to find Dinosaurs.
Part I: Geography

Dinosaurs have been found on every continent on Earth, even in Antarctica! This map shows where the dinosaurs in this book have been found.

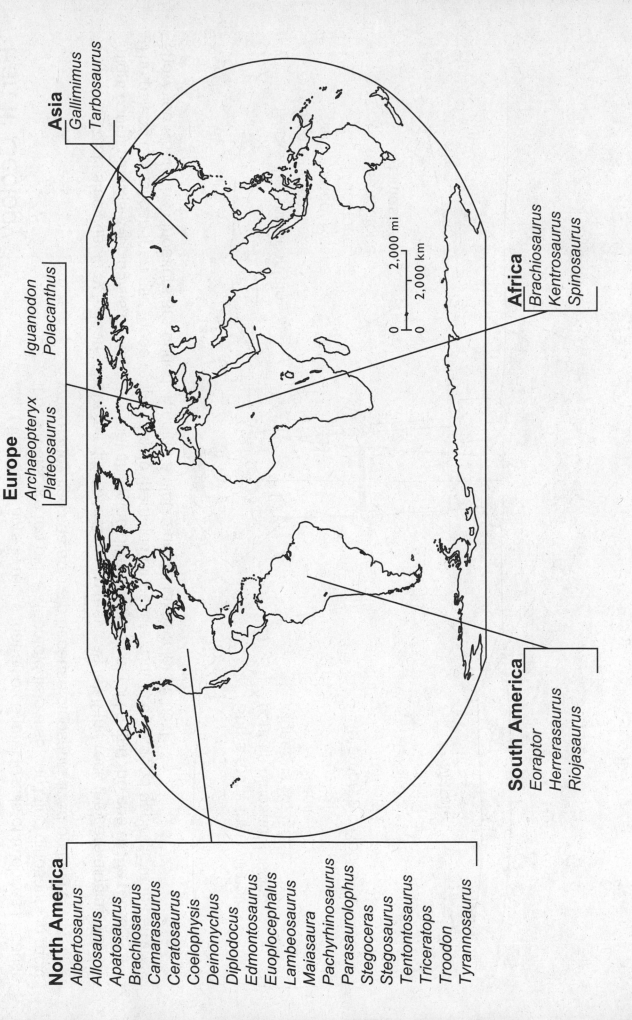

Asia
Gallimimus
Tarbosaurus

Europe
Archaeopteryx *Iguanodon*
Plateosaurus *Polacanthus*

Africa
Brachiosaurus
Kentrosaurus
Spinosaurus

2,000 mi
2,000 km
0
0

North America
Albertosaurus
Allosaurus
Apatosaurus
Brachiosaurus
Camarasaurus
Ceratosaurus
Coelophysis
Deinonychus
Diplodocus
Edmontosaurus
Euoplocephalus
Lambeosaurus
Maiasaura
Pachyrhinosaurus
Parasaurolophus
Stegoceras
Stegosaurus
Tentontosaurus
Triceratops
Troodon
Tyrannosaurus

South America
Eoraptor
Herrerasaurus
Riojasaurus

Where to find Dinosaurs.
Part II: Geology

Dinosaur fossils can only be found in certain types of rocks. The rock has to be the right age and of the right type. For example, paleontologists can't find dinosaurs in rocks that also contain fossils of trilobites because those rocks are too old. Paleontologists also can't find dinosaurs in rocks where they find sea animals because dinosaurs lived on land.

Paleontologists study geology to learn about the different rocks so they can tell if the rock they are digging in might contain fossils. Geologists make maps that show the different types of rocks and the age of the rocks. The paleontologist can then use these maps to help them find dinosaurs. But even a good geologic map can't show you where the dinosaurs are buried. Finding a dinosaur still takes a lot of luck!

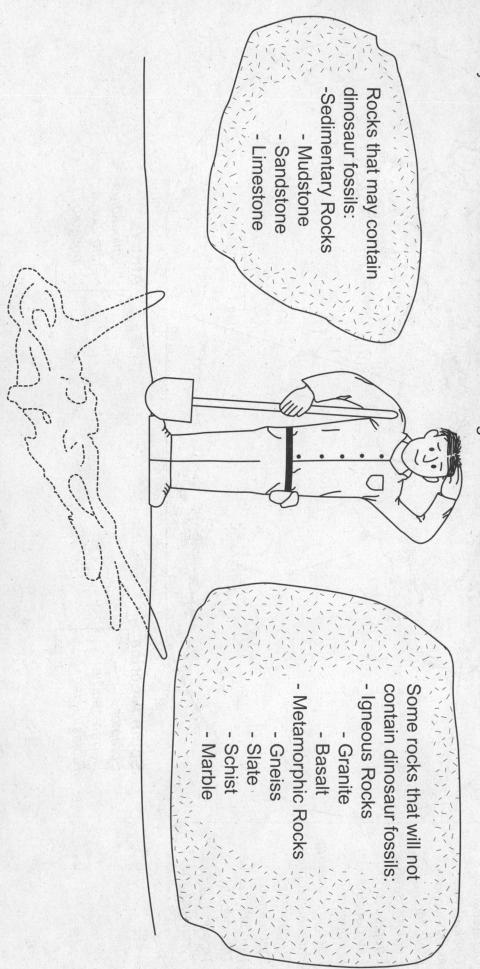

Rocks that may contain dinosaur fossils:
-Sedimentary Rocks
  - Mudstone
  - Sandstone
  - Limestone

Some rocks that will not contain dinosaur fossils:
- Igneous Rocks
  - Granite
  - Basalt
- Metamorphic Rocks
  - Gneiss
  - Slate
  - Schist
  - Marble

When to find Dinosaurs
Geologic Time Scale

The Earth is 4.6 BILLION years old. Dinosaurs have only lived for a small portion of this time.

Non-bird dinosaurs lived during the MESOZOIC ERA. To find a dinosaur a paleontologist must look at rocks that are of Mesozoic age.

Non-bird dinosaurs went extinct 65 million years ago.

The first birds evolved from small carnivorous dinosaurs 150 million years ago.

The earliest mammal fossils have been dated to over 200 million years ago.

The first dinosaur fossils have been dated to around 230 million years ago.

The first multi-cellular life appeared over 570 million years ago (Ma).

Eon	Era	Period	
Phanerozoic	Cenozoic	Neogene	Present
			23 Ma
		Paleogene	
			65 Ma
	Mesozoic	Cretaceous	
			146 Ma
		Jurassic	
			199 Ma
		Triassic	
			251 Ma
	Paleozoic	Permian	
			299 Ma
		Pennsylvanian	
			318 Ma
		Mississippian	
			359 Ma
		Devonian	
			416 Ma
		Silurian	
			443 Ma
		Ordovician	
			488 Ma
		Cambrian	
			542 Ma
Precambrian Eon			4600 Ma

Time Scale based on the International Stratigraphic Chart, 2004.

Deep Time

So how old is the Earth? We can say that the Earth formed 4.6 BILLION years ago, or that dinosaurs walked the Earth for 180 MILLION years, but what do these numbers mean?

How long is a million years? A simple way to think about how old the Earth is is to use a known amount of time to compare it to.

One way to compare geologic time is to think of all of Earth's history taking place in one 24-hour day. On this 'Earth Day' clock, the Precambrian Eon takes up the first 20 hours, starting at midnight and going until 8pm. The Paleozoic Era lasts for only 2 hours, ending at 10 pm. The Mesozoic Era, the Age of the Dinosaurs, lasts for only 1 hour and 15 minutes, ending at 11:15 pm. Finally, the Cenozoic Era takes up just the last 45 minutes of the day.

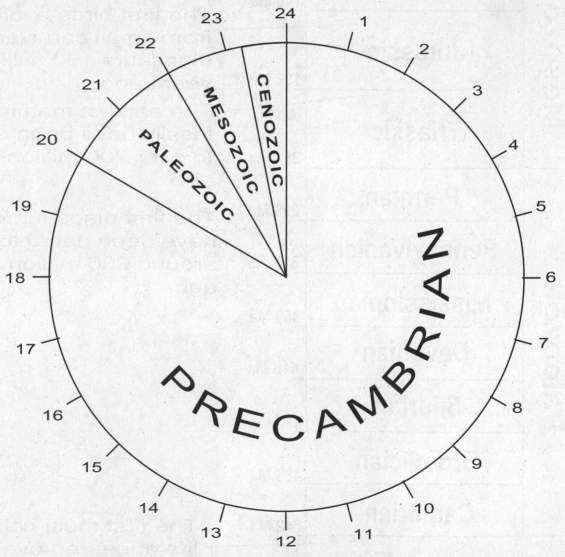

The 'Earth Day' Clock

DINOSAUR NEIGHBORS

Many other animals lived during the **Mesozoic Era** that were not dinosaurs.

Some of these non-dinosaur animals lived in the oceans. As a group they are usually called **marine reptiles**. They are related to modern reptiles. Examples of these animals include *mosasaurs*, *ichthyosaurs*, and *plesiosaurs*.

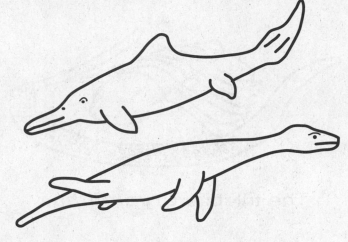

Other non-dinosaur animals could fly through the air. These animals are the **pterosaurs** and include animals like *Pteranodon*, *Dimorphodon*, and *Quetzalcoatlus* one of the largest animals to have ever flown!

The earliest mammals were small, no larger than a medium-size dog. Many were nocternal, which means they only came out at night. Some were big enough to feed on small dinosaurs!

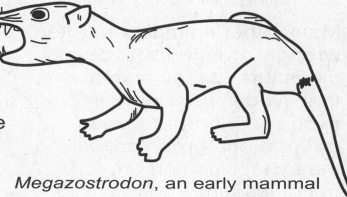

Megazostrodon, an early mammal

Many other types of animals lived during the time of the dinosaurs. These include insects, the earliest snakes, lizards, turtles, and the first birds. All of these animals helped to shape the world in which the dinosaurs lived.

WE'RE NOT DINOSAURS!

Many other animals lived before and after the dinosaurs lived.

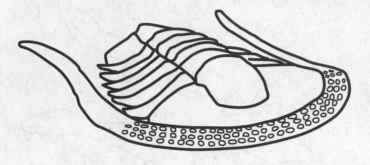

The trilobite *Cryptolithus*

Animals like the **trilobites** lived in the oceans from the Cambrian to the Permian Period and went extinct before the first dinosaurs lived.

Other animals were the main animals of their time, like the **placoderms**, or armored fishes. They lived in the Devonian Period.

The armored fish *Bothriolepis*

Many other animals are often wrongly grouped with the dinosaurs. Many animals that lived in the Permian, such as *Edaphosaurus*, are part of a group called the synapsids and are not dinosaurs.

The synapsid *Edaphosaurus*

The Dinosaur Skeleton

Paleontologists spend years studying the bones of dinosaurs. By knowing the different types of bones, a paleontologist can easily identify a bone they find in the field. They can even tell which animal the bone belongs to.

Here are the basic parts of the dinosaur skeleton.

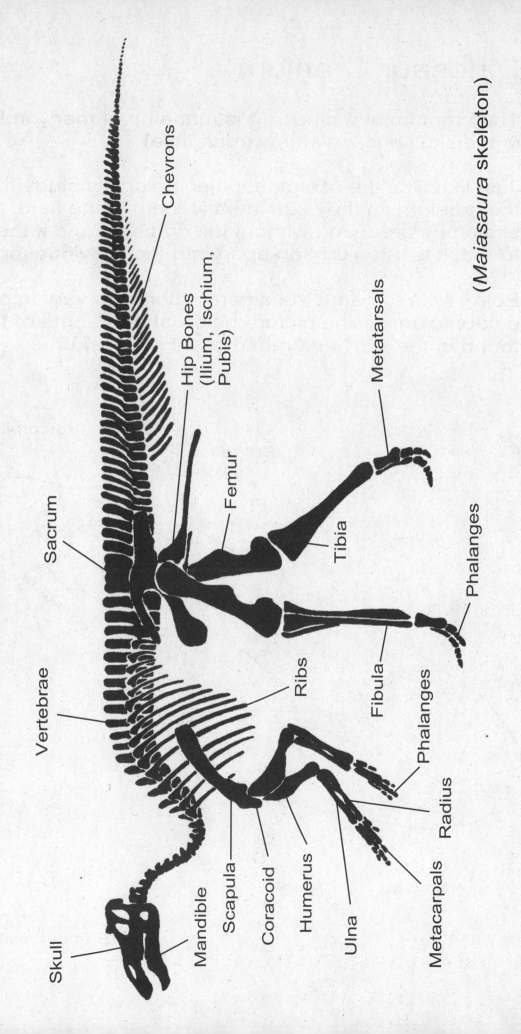

(*Maiasaura* skeleton)

Chevrons

Hip Bones (Ilium, Ischium, Pubis)

Femur

Metatarsals

Tibia

Phalanges

Sacrum

Fibula

Phalanges

Vertebrae

Ribs

Radius

Skull

Mandible

Scapula

Coracoid

Humerus

Ulna

Metacarpals

Dinosaur Cranium

The cranium of a dinosaur is made up of many individual bones in the skull and lower jaw (mandible).

Just like with the skeleton, paleontologists study the bones of the cranium so they can identify them in the field. Most dinosaur skeletons are found without the cranium, and if the cranium is found, it is often broken apart into the individual bones.

Being able to name the different bones is very important to the paleontologist. The picture below shows some of the bones found in the skull and mandible of a dinosaur.

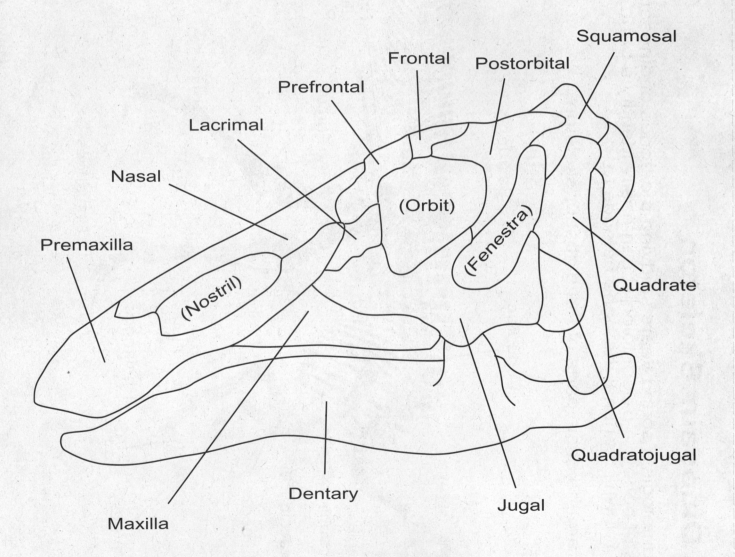

(*Edmontosaurus* skull)

Dinosaur Teeth - Herbivores

Along with looking for dinosaur bones, paleontologists also look for dinosaur teeth. Sometimes, when looking for dinosaurs the only fossils a paleontologist finds are the teeth of a dinosaur.

Dinosaur teeth can tell the paleontologist a lot about a dinosaur. Different dinosaurs have differently shaped teeth. By looking at the tooth, the paleontologist can tell what kind of dinosaur lost the tooth. They can even tell what kind of food the dinosaur ate and how they ate it.

Herbivorous dinosaurs (plant-eaters) have many different types of teeth. Their teeth are specially designed for eating certain types of plants. Below are four examples of herbivorous dinosaurs and the shape of their teeth.

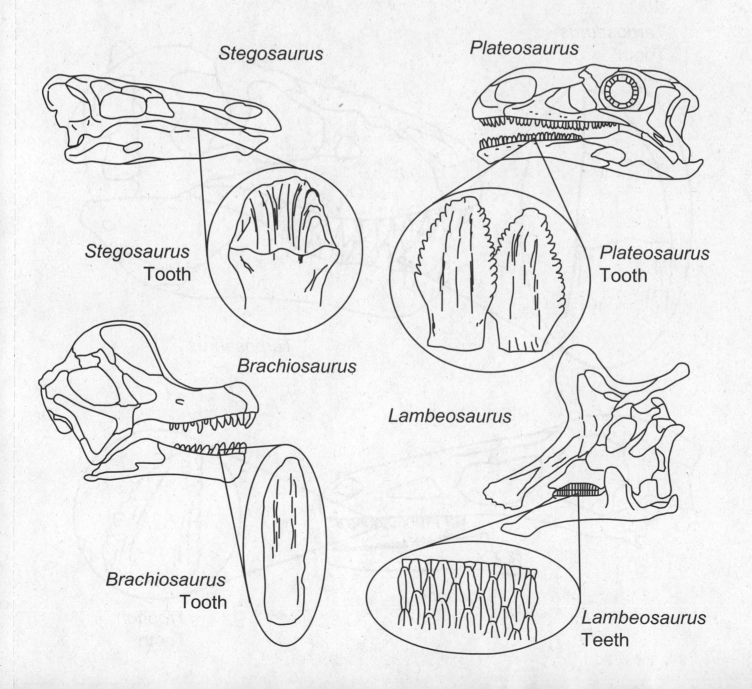

Stegosaurus

Plateosaurus

Stegosaurus Tooth

Plateosaurus Tooth

Brachiosaurus

Lambeosaurus

Brachiosaurus Tooth

Lambeosaurus Teeth

Dinosaur Teeth - Carnivores

Probably the most identifiable of dinosaur teeth are those that belonged to the carnivorous (meat-eating) dinosaurs. These teeth are often described as being knife- or dagger-shaped and they can easily cut through meat.

Even among carnivorous dinosaurs there are different tooth shapes. Just like in herbivorous dinosaurs, paleontologists can sometimes identify the species of a carnivorous dinosaur from looking at their teeth. Many carnivorous dinosaurs lost their teeth when they ate their prey, so sometimes a paleontologist can tell what kind of animals fed on a dinosaur from the presence of carnivore teeth.

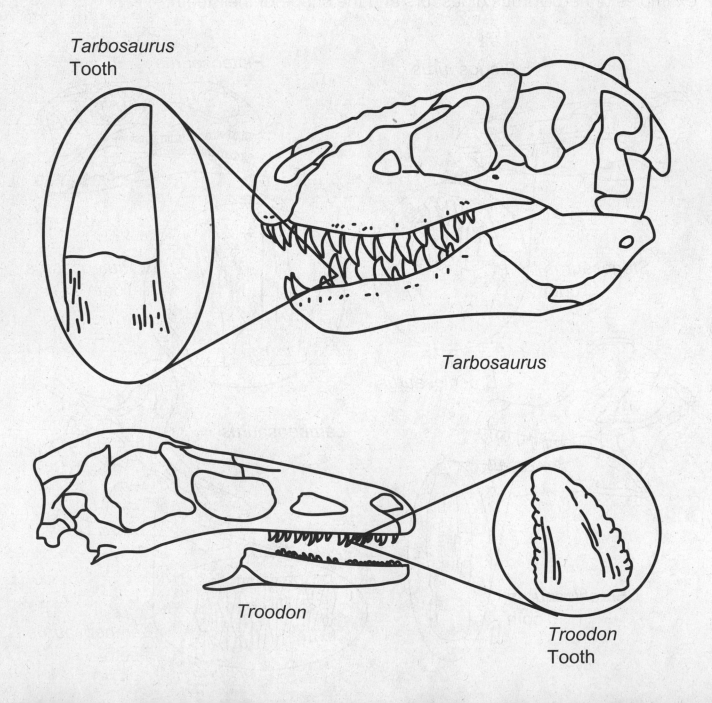

Tarbosaurus Tooth

Tarbosaurus

Troodon

Troodon Tooth

Frills, Horns, and Armor: Part I - Skulls

Some dinosaurs have wild and strange looking skulls. These skulls can have horns, broad frills covering the neck, or helmet-like crests.

Paleontologists still debate the exact function of these ornaments. Some were probably used for defense, and others may have been used to protect the dinosaur. Others may have been used to attract female dinosaurs or to scare male dinosaurs. We may never know, but these different skulls make it easy to name the different dinosaurs.

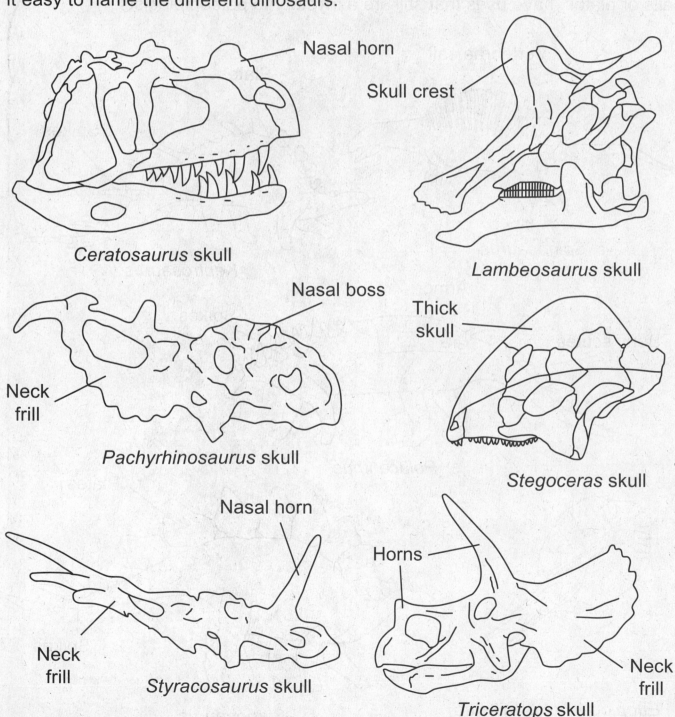

Nasal horn

Ceratosaurus skull

Skull crest

Lambeosaurus skull

Nasal boss

Neck frill

Pachyrhinosaurus skull

Thick skull

Stegoceras skull

Nasal horn

Neck frill

Styracosaurus skull

Horns

Neck frill

Triceratops skull

Frills, Horns, and Armor: Part II - Bodies

Along with strange looking skulls, many dinosaurs also had strange looking bodies. These included tall sails on their backs, plates and spikes, and bony armor.

For some dinosaurs the use of their ornaments, like armor, are clear; they protected the dinosaur from attack. Some ornaments may have been used to defend the dinosaur, like tail clubs and spikes. Other ornaments, like tall sails or plates, have uses that still are a mystery to paleontologists.

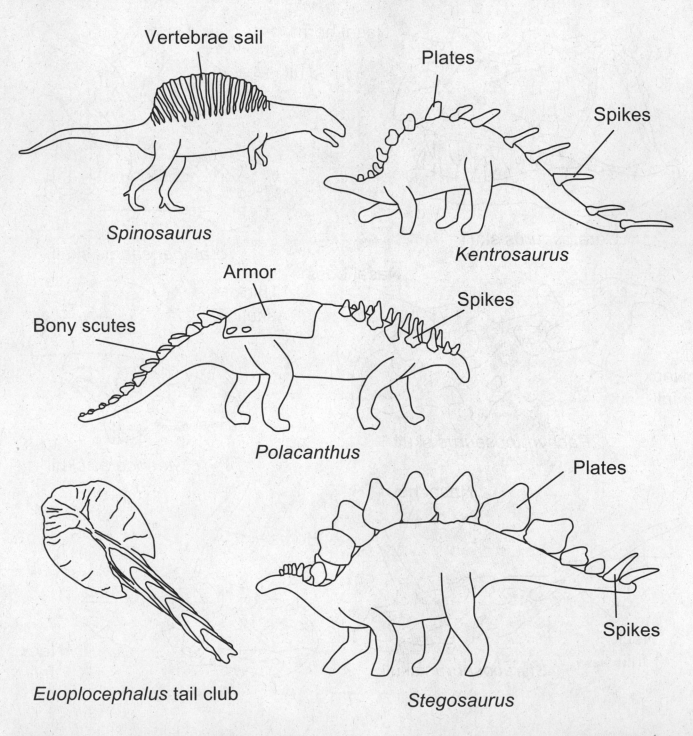

Vertebrae sail

Spinosaurus

Plates

Spikes

Kentrosaurus

Armor

Bony scutes

Spikes

Polacanthus

Euoplocephalus tail club

Plates

Spikes

Stegosaurus

The Triassic

Period	Epoch	Age	
TRIASSIC			200 MA
	Late	Rhaetian	204 MA
		Norian	217 MA
		Carnian	228 MA
	Middle	Ladinian	237 MA
		Anisian	245 MA
	Early	Olenekian	250 MA
		Induan	251 MA

Stratigraphic Chart after International Startigraphic Chart, 2004

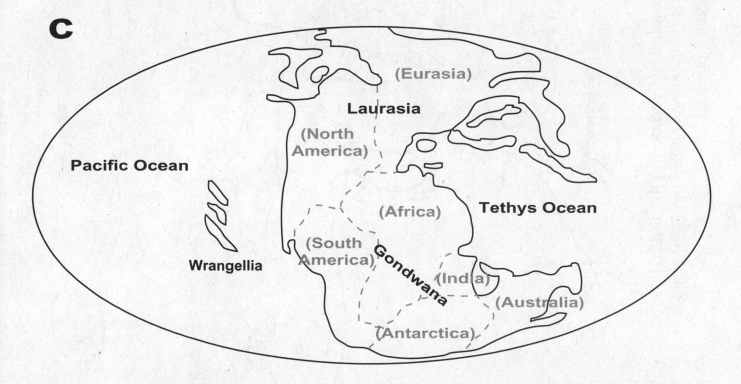

The Triassic Globe (220 MA)

Coelophysis ("Hollow Form") was a small, carnivorous dinosaur that lived during the Late Triassac in North America. Its name comes from the animal's hollow, bird-like bones. Although *Coelophysis* was an early dinosaur, it shared many other features with modern birds.

Some of the first dinosaurs were *Herrerasaurus* ("Herrera's Lizard") and *Eoraptor* ("Dawn Hunter"). Both lived during the Late Triassic period and their fossils have been found in South America. Both were carnivores.

Eoraptor

Herrerasaurus

DINOSAUR WORD SEARCH

```
D B F H J L N B A C E G I A K M O Q S U W Y B S I E V J T D C
Q T L E V E O R A P T O R R T N H O N B A P O T S V U R U S T
C F I L E A R A P T O R O R E U E X A D G A J E M O R U N Q W
N P R S S R I C H T H Y O S A U R R U S O R M G E N P S V Y L
E V D B G I C H T H I O S A U R R U S C P A T O Z I C L N G D
U W Y A C E G I K M O Q S U H W E H K M Q S T S M Q K H S L P
S T I G U A N O D O N A E S A U R U S D L A I A S P N D O N Y
R A C A E D L S Q N I A T L C A M A R A S A U R U S P Z H J D
L O L L I N E A P Z I C F G H O S N A P E R I R G S J D I K S
L P N L G O E U O P L O C E P H A L U S C O A U T E D I V P I
A J L I B E R R T O S E A U R I U U S A L L L S S A U P U K U
S U A M U R I U S C H R I A W N R S O U U O T A M L E L R D C
O R N I T H I S C H I A N T L A U N G R O P O M E S O Z O I C
G A R M A P E F R U I T T A R N S D L I E H M O A R D D E P R
N S I U C E T O D R I O N K N E A T O S T U R I C E R O A L O
H S O S T Y R A C O S A U R U S W O D C A S B O U T U C S O N
O I T H E R D I N O S A A U R S H I A H T I T N P G R U E D K
H C R Y P T O C L E I D U S A D E T R I C E R A T O P S O O U
R U S V E E L O C I R R A P T O R Y P A R O I T E O C E R C T
M P S T H N E T Y T A U N A T Y R A N N O S A U R U S I C U U
A K A L L O S A U R U S S T R N E R L D W A S R A S B E L S I
I S E I S N M O S A U R U S P A R A S A B I S G N A N I M D N
A L B E R T O S A U R U S R N A A N T O D E I N O N Y C H U S
S S E N E O T D O R N P R N T Q S W Y S I R C E D L A V E N T
A D A N G S T E G O C E R A S E A L O U N S L Y O A N K Y L O
U A U G R A U S O F U R A S N O U E L A O U R U N S U T A P H
R A P T O U R M H O N O D C L O R F N I S U S N C I U D A D C
A R L Y C R E T A C E O U S T H U S A U A U F R U T S L A R M
S I O S A U U O R U S V C E N T S L R O U S A U R U S D T I T
N O O S A S U R U I S C E N P I H D C E R A T O S A U R U S A
```

Find the following dinosaur names and other terms in the puzzle above.

Tentontosaurs	*Stegosaurus*	*Brachiosaurus*
Camarasaurus	*Tyrannosaurus*	*Diplodocus*
Ichthyosaurus	*Deinonychus*	*Albertosaurus*
Gallimimus	*Ornithischian*	*Herrerasaurus*
Euoplocephalus	*Eoraptor*	*Iguanodon*
Parasaurolophus	*Stegoceras*	*Cryptocleidus*
Saurischian	*Maiasaura*	*Allosaurus*
Pteranodon	*Triceratops*	*Styracosaurus*
Ceratosaurus	Cretaceous	Jurassic
Triassic	Mesozoic	Dinosaur

Riojasaurus

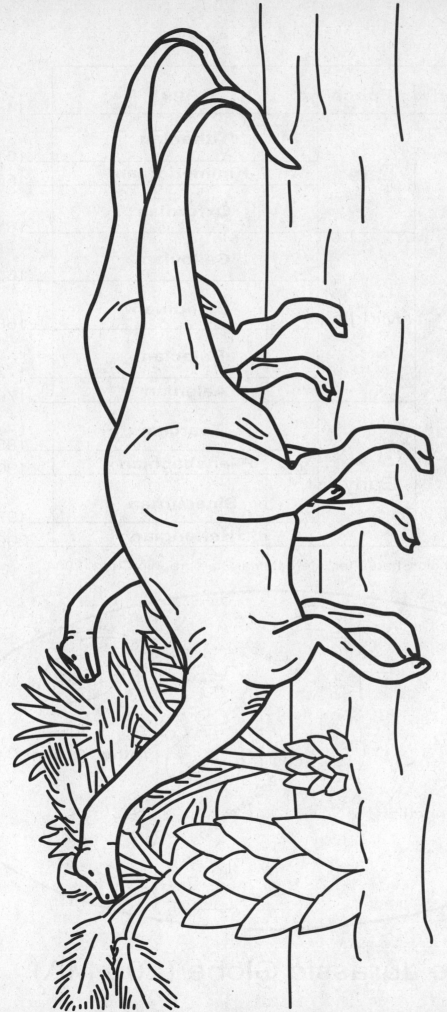

Riojasaurus ("La Rioja Lizard") is a prosauropod dinosaur. These animals lived during the Late Triassic and may have shared a common ancestor with the sauropod dinosaurs. Prosauropods were some of the first really big dinosaurs, growing to over 30 feet in length. *Riojasaurus* was a herbivore and lived in South America.

The Jurassic

Period	Epoch	Age	
			146 MA
J U R A S S I C	Late	Tithonian	
			151 MA
		Kimmeridgian	
			156 MA
		Oxfordian	
			161 MA
	Middle	Callovian	
			165 MA
		Bathonian	
			168 MA
		Bajocian	
			172 MA
		Aalenian	
			176 MA
	Early	Toarcian	
			183 MA
		Pliensbachian	
			190 MA
		Sinemurian	
			197 MA
		Hettangian	
			200 MA

Stratigraphic Chart after International Startigraphic Chart, 2004

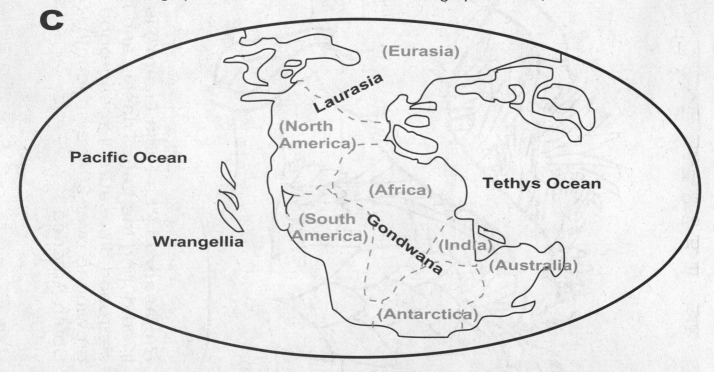

The Jurassic Globe (200 MA)

Allosaurus

Allosaurus ("Other Lizard") was the top predator in North America during the Late Jurassic. It was a skilled predator and mostly hunted alone. There is evidence from a quarry in Utah that groups of allosaurs may have gathered together.

Dinosaur connect-the-dots!

Follow the alphabet to fill in the shape of the dinosaur.

This dinosaur lived in Africa during the Late Jurassic period. It was a herbivore and its name means 'Arm Lizard.' Can you name this dinosaur?

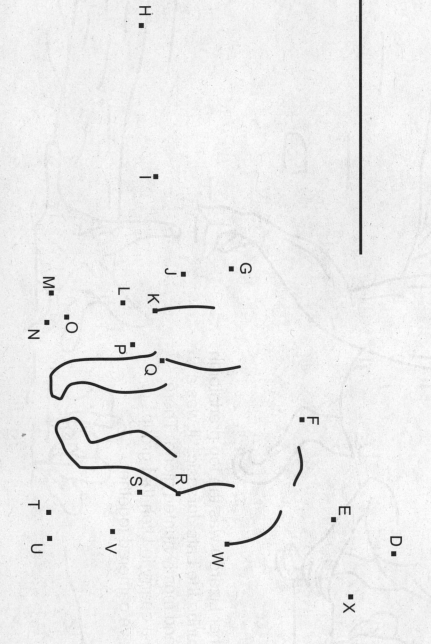

The wrong skull, based on the skull of *Camarasaurus*, had been displayed on skeletons for nearly 100 years.

The name **Apatosaurus** ("Deceptive Reptile") is quite appropriate for this dinosaur given the confusion surrounding it. For many years the animal was incorrectly named *Brontosaurus* and skeletons in museums around the world showed the animal with the wrong feet and skull!

Apatosaurus

The confusion began in the 1870's when *Apatosaurus* was discovered and named by O. C. Marsh. The skeleton was found without a skull. When scientists put the skeleton together they used a skull that had been found nearby, thinking it was the right one. It wasn't until the 1970's that the mistake was corrected. Today we know that *Apatosaurus* is a diplodocid sauropod and had a long whip-like tail and a small narrow head.

The correct skull for *Apatosaurus*, identified finally in 1975.

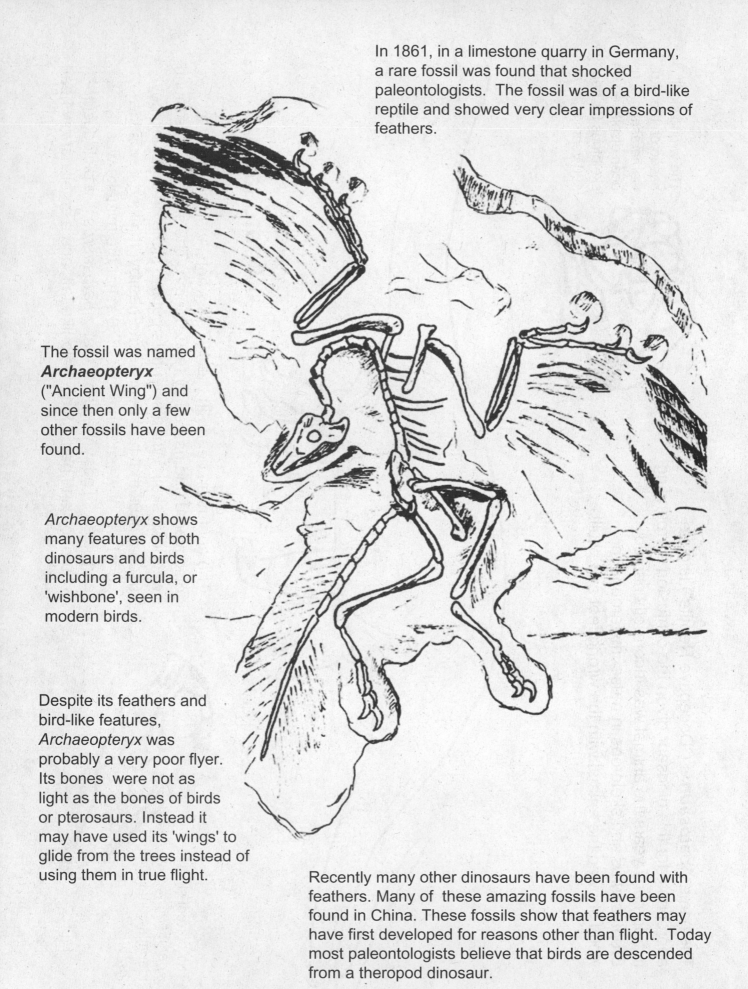

In 1861, in a limestone quarry in Germany, a rare fossil was found that shocked paleontologists. The fossil was of a bird-like reptile and showed very clear impressions of feathers.

The fossil was named *Archaeopteryx* ("Ancient Wing") and since then only a few other fossils have been found.

Archaeopteryx shows many features of both dinosaurs and birds including a furcula, or 'wishbone', seen in modern birds.

Despite its feathers and bird-like features, *Archaeopteryx* was probably a very poor flyer. Its bones were not as light as the bones of birds or pterosaurs. Instead it may have used its 'wings' to glide from the trees instead of using them in true flight.

Recently many other dinosaurs have been found with feathers. Many of these amazing fossils have been found in China. These fossils show that feathers may have first developed for reasons other than flight. Today most paleontologists believe that birds are descended from a theropod dinosaur.

One of the largest sauropods, **Brachiosaurus** ("Arm Lizard") fossils have been found in North America and in Africa. *Brachiosaurus* was a herbivore and lived during the Late Jurassic period.

Brachiosaurus

Which is the dinosaur?

Somebody mixed up the models of the prehistoric animals. Can you help the paleontologist sort the animals into the correct groups: dinosaurs and non-dinosaurs.

Draw a line from the animal to the correct group.

Non-Dinosaurs

Dinosaurs

Camarasaurus ("Chambered Lizard") lived in North America during the Late Jurassic period. They had a short, deep skull and a shorter neck and tail than other sauropods like *Diplodocus*. *Camarasaurus* was a herbivore.

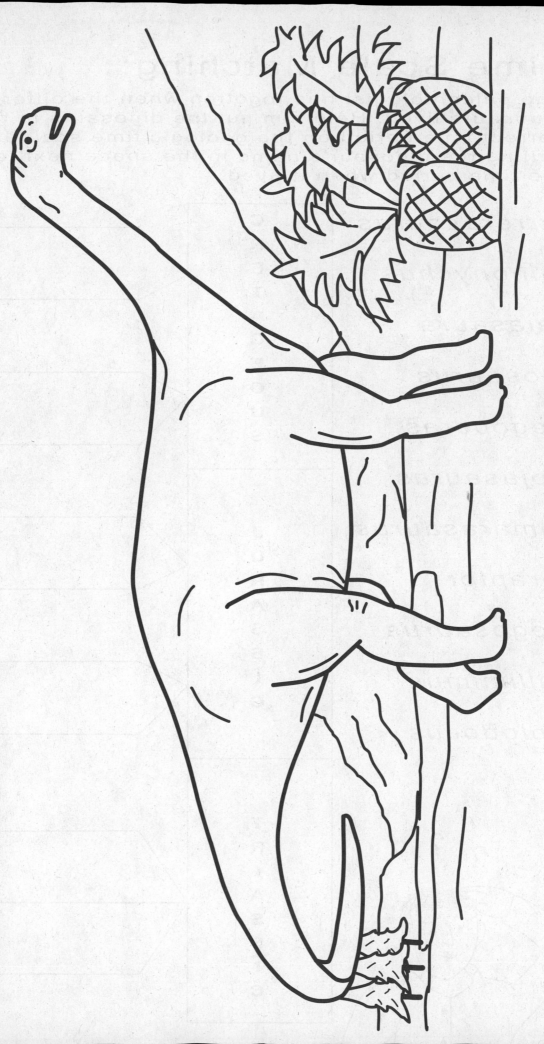

Camarasaurus

Time Scale Matching:

The paleontologist has fogotten when the different dinosaurs lived. Help him put the dinosaurs in their correct time period on the geologic time scale by writing the dinosaur's name in the space next to the time period when it lived.

Herrerasaurus

Deinonychus

Maiasaura

Allosaurus

Stegoceras

Riojasaurus

Camarasaurus

Eoraptor

Stegosaurus

Gallimimus

Diplodocus

CRETACEOUS

JURASSIC

TRIASSIC

? ? ?

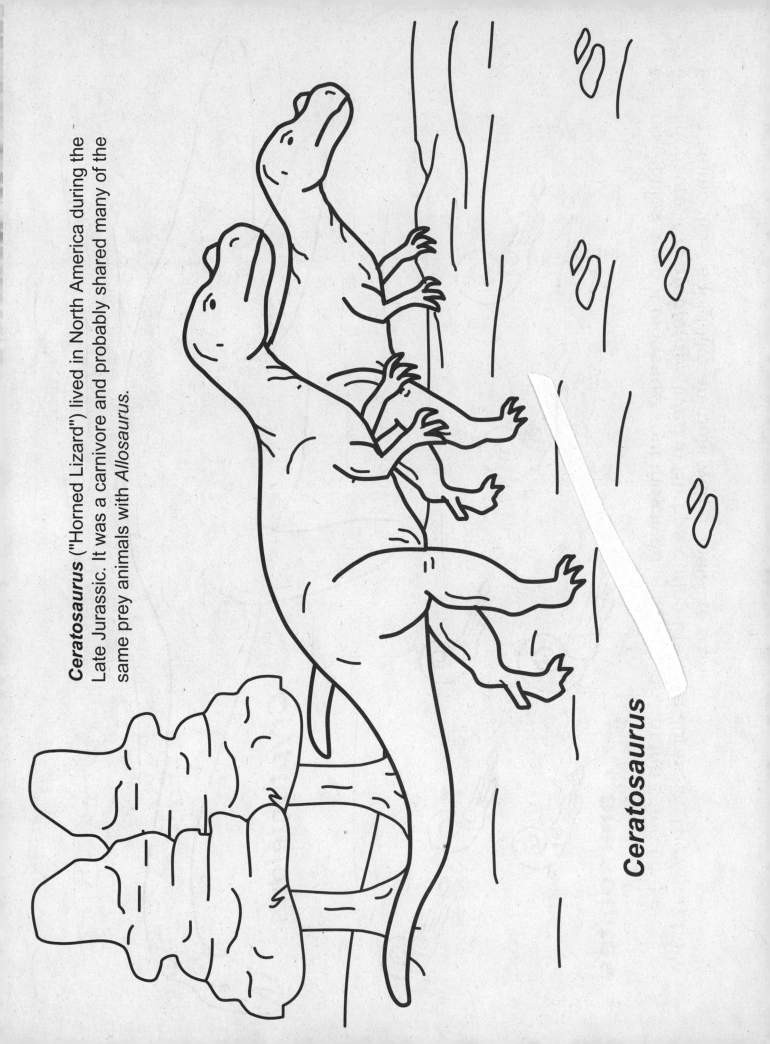

Ceratosaurus ("Horned Lizard") lived in North America during the Late Jurassic. It was a carnivore and probably shared many of the same prey animals with *Allosaurus*.

Ceratosaurus

Marine reptiles are not dinosaurs, but they lived in the oceans at the same time as the dinosaurs. **Cryptocleidus** lived in Europe during the Late Jurassic. They may have fed on ammonites; squid-like animals with a shell like a snail.

ammonites

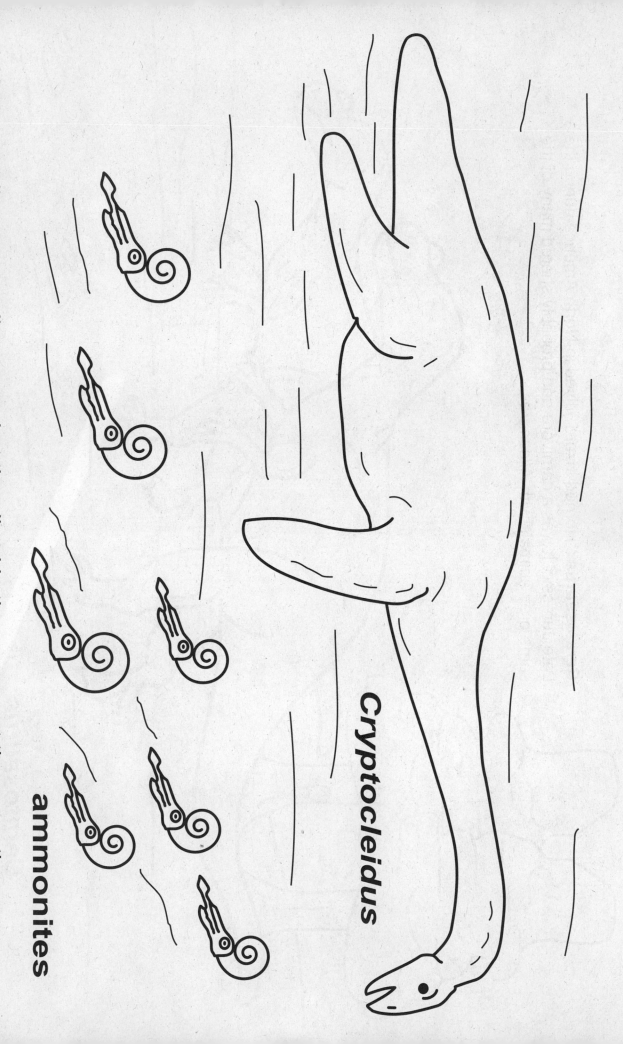

Cryptocleidus

Dinosaur Dentistry!

Help the paleontologist match up the correct tooth with the correct dinosaur skull. Draw a line between the tooth and the skull.

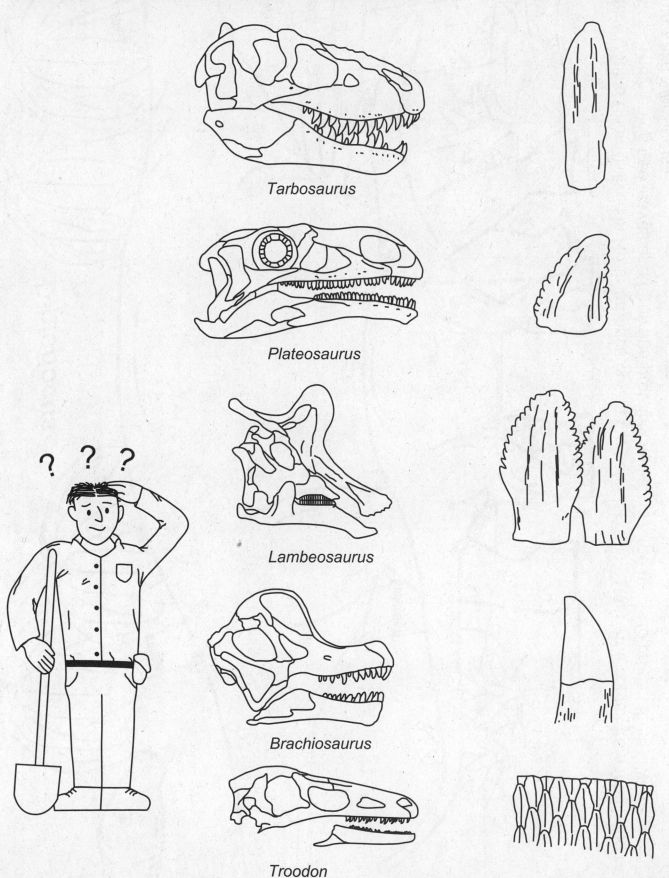

Tarbosaurus

Plateosaurus

Lambeosaurus

Brachiosaurus

Troodon

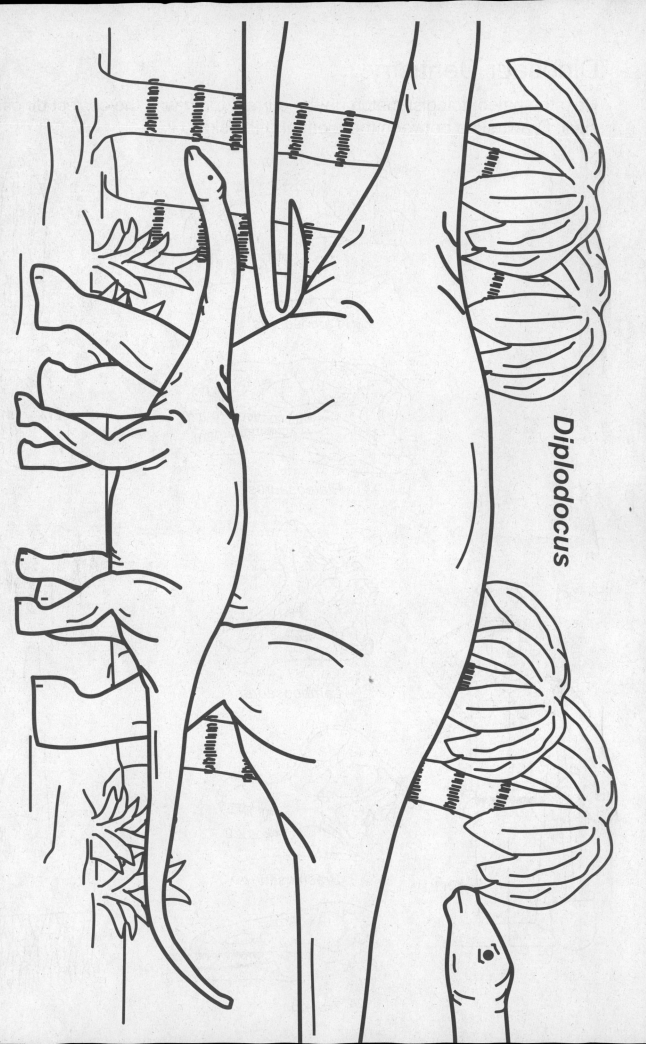

Diplodocus

Diplodocus ("Double Beam") lived in North America during the Late Jurassic. The name comes from the shape of the tail bones. They fed on tree leaves and ferns and probably moved in large herds to protect themselves from predators like *Allosaurus*.

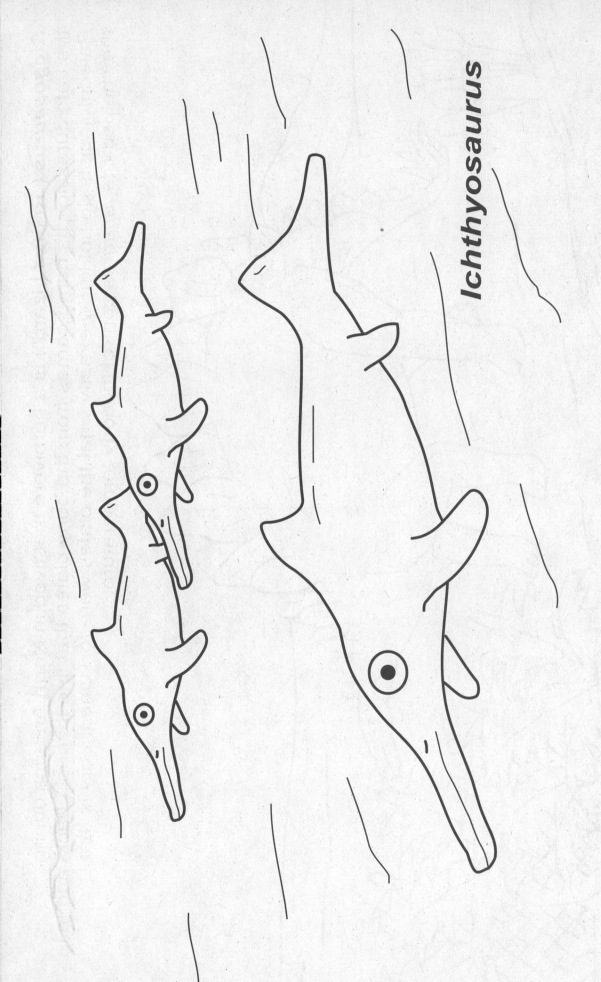

Ichthyosaurus

Ichthyosaurus ("Fish Lizard") looked like modern dolphins and lived in Europe and North America during the Middle Jurassic. Ichthyosaurs are not dinosaurs; they are marine reptiles and they fed on fish.

Stegosaurus ("Roofed Lizard") is a herbivore that lived in North America during the Late Jurassic. Its name comes from the bony plates that line its neck, back, and tail. Paleontologists do not know exactly what the plates were for. One theory is that they helped Stegosaurus control its body temperature.

Stegosaurus

DINOSAUR DEFINITIONS

Fill in the correct answer for each question. Then take the letter from the box in each answer to spell out the answer to the question at the bottom of the page.

The name of this flying reptile mean "wing tooth".

☐ __ __ __ __ __ __ __ __ __ __

This dinosaur is a "good mother lizard" and used to live in Montana.

__ __ __ ☐ __ __ __ __ __ __

This Late Jurassic dinosaur is often mistaken for *Tyrannosaurus rex* but this "other lizard" has three fingers on its hands.

__ __ ☐ __ __ __ __ __ __ __

The non-bird dinosaurs went extinct 65 million years ago at the end of this geologic time period.

__ __ __ __ __ __ __ ☐ __ __ __

This long necked herbivores name means "double beam".

__ __ __ __ ☐ __ __ __ __ __ __

Although its name means "bird hip", birds are not descended from this type of dinosaur.

__ __ ☐ __ __ __ __ __ __ __ __ __ __

This Late Triassic carnivore's name means "dawn hunter", and it was one of the earliest true dinosaurs.

__ __ __ __ __ ☐ __ __

This Late Cretaceous duck-billed dinosaur had a long skull and may have been able to make "hooting" noises.

__ __ __ __ ☐ __ __ __ __ __ __ __

This Late Cretaceous carnivore's name means "chicken mimic".

__ __ __ __ ☐ __ __ __ __ __ __

This Late Jurassic herbivore's name means "roofed lizard".

__ __ __ __ ☐ __ __ __ __ __ __

This dinosaur was one of the first to be discovered and its name means "iguana tooth".

__ __ ☐ __ __ __ __ __ __ __

This marine reptile lived during the Middle Jurassic.

__ __ __ __ ☐ __ __ __ __ __ __

Fill in the letters from above to answer this question.

What do you call the study of ancient animals and their fossils?

__ __ __ __ __ __ __ __ __ __ __ __ __ __

The Cretaceous

Period	Epoch	Age	
C R E T A C E O U S	Late		65.5 MA
		Maastrichtian	
			71 MA
		Campanian	
			84 MA
		Santonian	86 MA
		Coniacian	89 MA
		Turonian	94 MA
		Cenomanian	
			100 MA
	Early	**Albian**	
			112 MA
		Aptian	
			125 MA
		Barremian	
			130 MA
		Hauterivian	
			136 MA
		Valanginian	
			140 MA
		Berriasian	
			146 MA

Stratigraphic Chart after International Startigraphic Chart, 2004

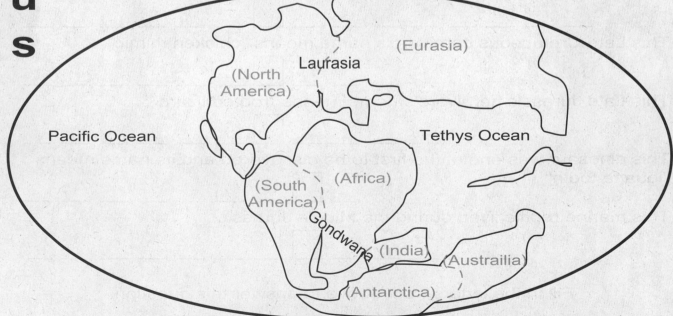

The Cretaceous Globe (130 MA)

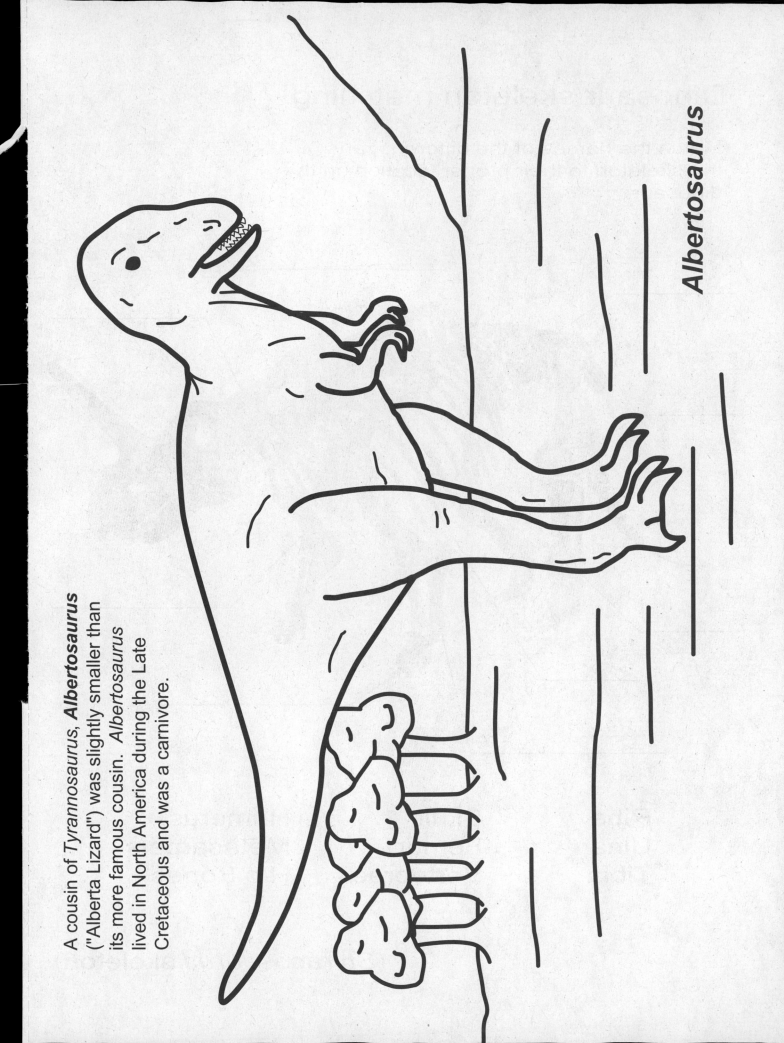

A cousin of *Tyrannosaurus*, **Albertosaurus** ("Alberta Lizard") was slightly smaller than its more famous cousin. *Albertosaurus* lived in North America during the Late Cretaceous and was a carnivore.

Albertosaurus

Dinosaur skeleton matching.

Match the names of the different parts of the skeleton to their proper location on the dinosaur.

Ribs   Skull   Humerus

Ulna   Femur   Metacarpals

Tibia   Vertebrae   Hip Bones

(*Styracosaurus* skeleton)

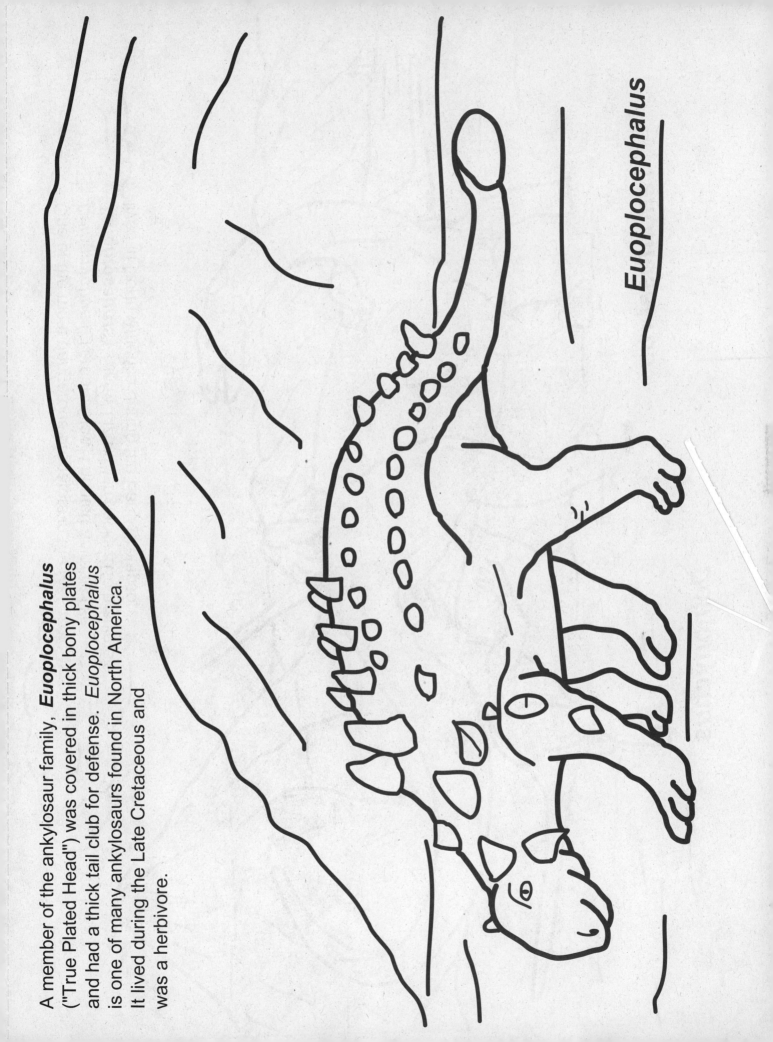

A member of the ankylosaur family, **Euoplocephalus** ("True Plated Head") was covered in thick bony plates and had a thick tail club for defense. *Euoplocephalus* is one of many ankylosaurs found in North America. It lived during the Late Cretaceous and was a herbivore.

Euoplocephalus

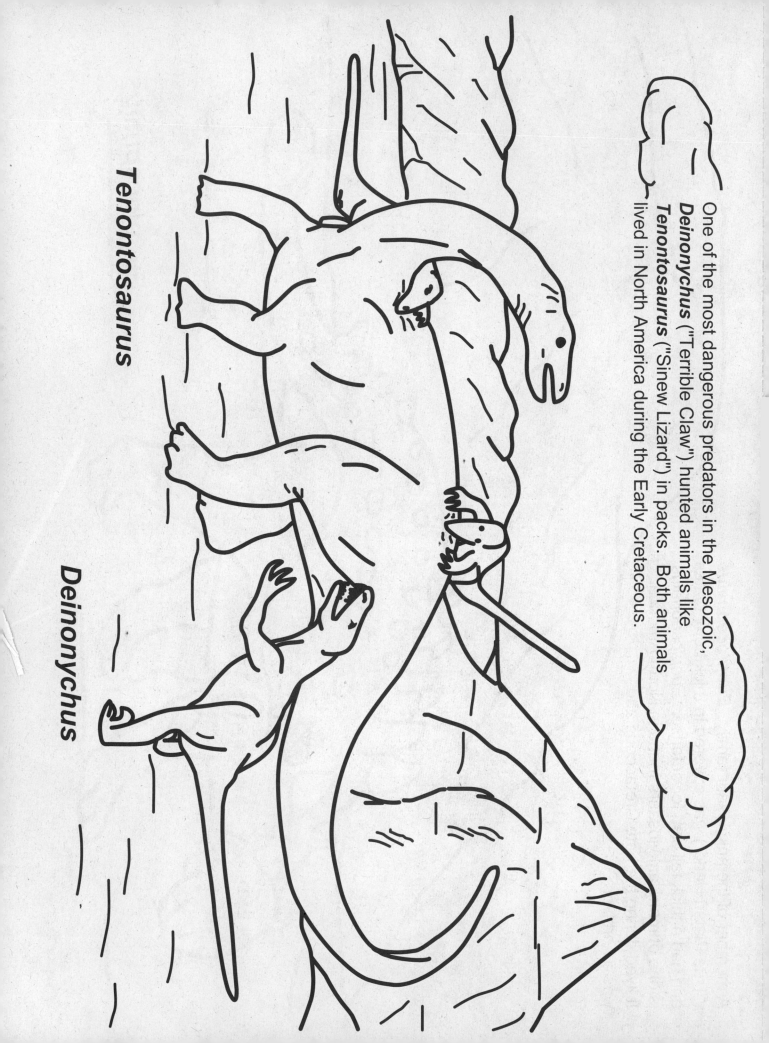

One of the most dangerous predators in the Mesozoic, *Deinonychus* ("Terrible Claw") hunted animals like *Tenontosaurus* ("Sinew Lizard") in packs. Both animals lived in North America during the Early Cretaceous.

Tenontosaurus

Deinonychus

DINOSAUR DEFINITIONS TWO

Fill in the correct answer for each question. Then take the letter
from the box in each answer to spell out the answer to the question
at the bottom of the page.

This "tyrant lizard" lived during the Late Cretaceous.

☐ _ _ _ _ _ _ _ _ _ _ _ _

This dinosaur was a prosauropod that lived in South America.

☐ _ _ _ _ _ _ _ _ _ _ _ _

This Late Cretaceous dinosaurs name means "three horn face".

_ _ ☐ _ _ _ _ _ _ _ _

For a long time this "deceptive reptile" was displayed in museums with the
wrong skull on its skeleton.

_ _ _ _ _ _ ☐ _ _ _ _

Another Late Cretaceous dinosaur of the family Ceratopsidae whose name
means "spiked lizard".

_ _ _ _ _ _ _ _ _ _ ☐

This North American dinosaur had a very thick skull and its name means
"horny roof".

☐ _ _ _ _ _ _ _ _ _ _

This Early Cretaceous dinosaur hunted its prey in packs.

_ _ ☐ _ _ _ _ _ _ _ _

One of the earliest dinosaurs, this dinosaur's name means "hollow form".

☐ _ _ _ _ _ _ _ _ _ _

Fill in the letters from above to answer this question.
In which geologic time period did the first dinosaurs live?

_ _ _ _ _ _ _ _

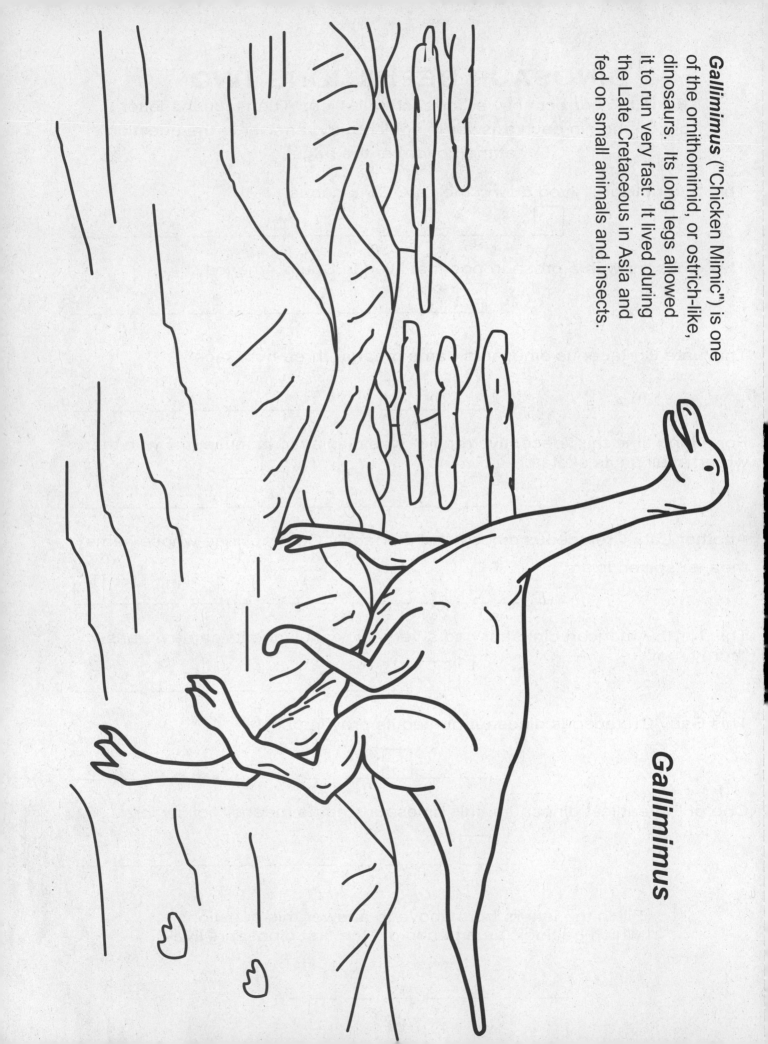

Gallimimus ("Chicken Mimic") is one of the ornithomimid, or ostrich-like, dinosaurs. Its long legs allowed it to run very fast. It lived during the Late Cretaceous in Asia and fed on small animals and insects.

Gallimimus

Dinosaur connect-the-dots!

Follow the alphabet to fill in the shape of
the dinosaur skull.

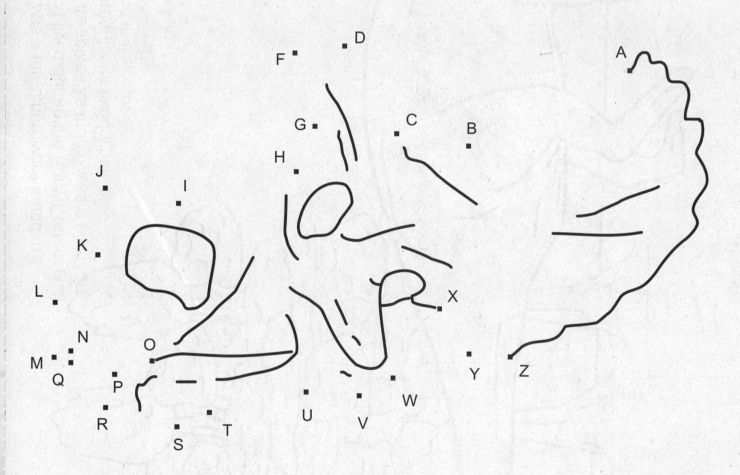

This herbivorous dinosaur lived in herds in
North America during the Late Cretaceous.
It's name means "Three-Horn Face". Can you
name this dinosaur?

_____

Iguanodon ("Iguana Tooth") was a large herbivore found in Europe and North America and lived during the Early Cretaceous. Paleontologists once thought its spike-like thumb was a horn on its nose. The wrong placement was fixed when complete skeletons were found in Belgium.

Iguanodon

Maiasaura ("Good Mother Lizard") is a hadrosaur, or duck-billed, dinosaur. It lived in North America during the Late Cretaceous. *Maiasaura* lived in large herds and built nests to lay their eggs. Paleontologists have learned that *Maiasaura*, and maybe other dinosaurs, returned to the same nesting grounds year after year.

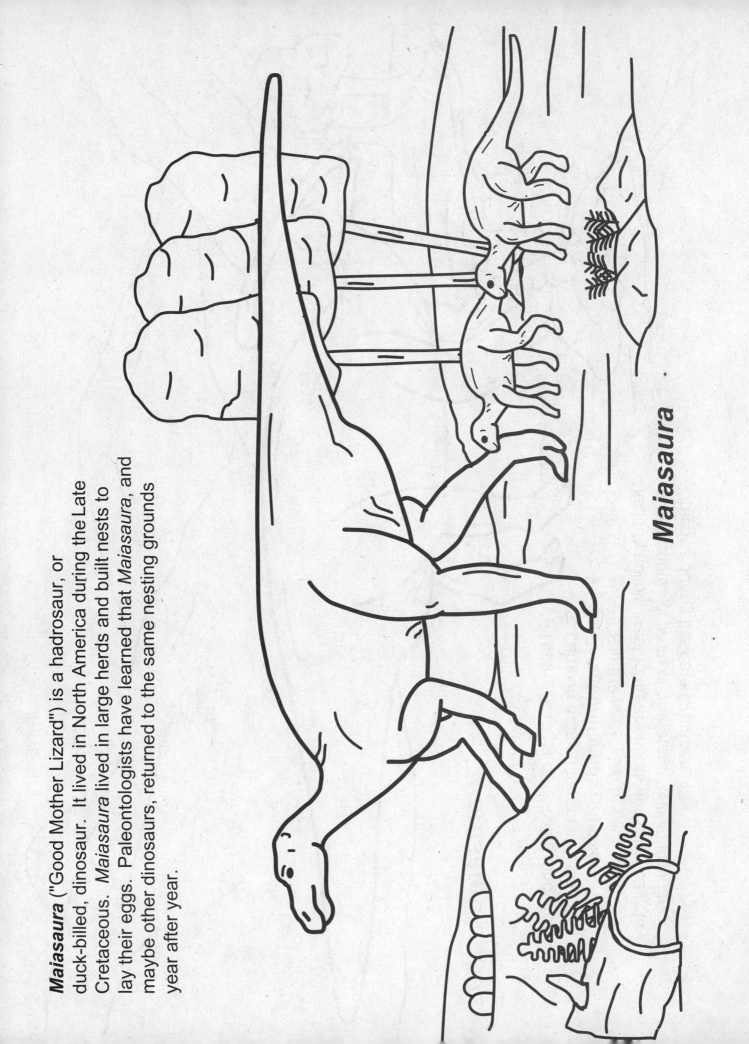

Maiasaura

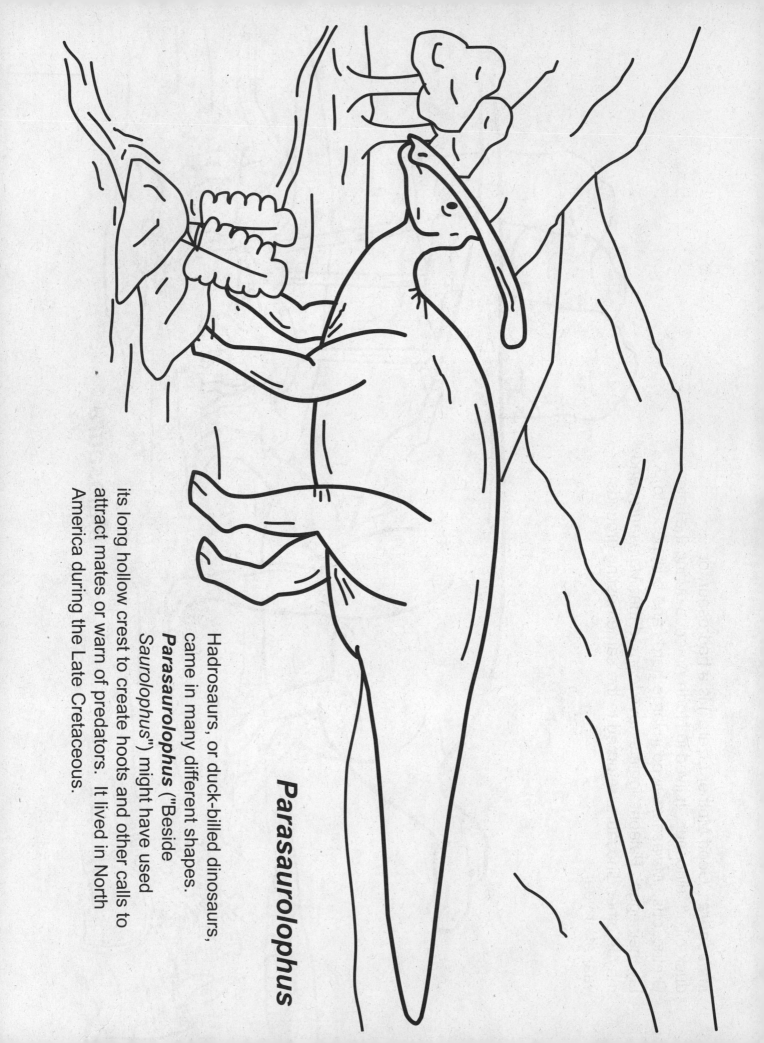

Parasaurolophus

Hadrosaurs, or duck-billed dinosaurs, came in many different shapes. *Parasaurolophus* ("Beside Saurolophus") might have used its long hollow crest to create hoots and other calls to attract mates or warn of predators. It lived in North America during the Late Cretaceous.

Pteranodon

The skies in the Mesozoic were filled with all types of flying reptiles, or pterosaurs. Pterosaurs were not dinosaurs, but were related to them.

One of the largest to fly in the air was *Pteranodon* ("Wing Tooth"). *Pteranodon* lived during the Late Cretaceous and its fossils are found in Europe and North America.

SECOND DINOSAUR WORD SEARCH

```
D P U B I S N D A C E K I K M O P S L L A B J S K E L E T O N
Q T L E P N D O E F I E K T N R I O J A S A U R U S R U S D T
C V E R T E B R A E R N O R U B X A L G H J I M O R U N Q P W
N P R S L R P Q N L J T F S P I N O S A U R U S N P S V Y L L
E V D B E C A W P W I R J H X A W V C P C T R Z I C L N G A D
T R O O D O N B K M S Q S U W R L K M Q L A X M Q K H S L T P
S T G O D O N O S A C S E A U C U E T R A T N I A P D O N E Y
R A C E E D L H Q N H A C A M H R A O L K A U T P Z H J N O D
L O L K I P E R P Z I U G H O A N A P N W R C G H J L I K S U
M P N V G A J K L Q U R D M Y E T O Y C T B U T S U H V P A Z
A G L I B L R R T O M R A U R O U S E L H O S O S P S U R U S
X E A N U E I U S L H T I A N P S O T U O S L A M A L R I R A
I R E D M O N T O S A U R U S T N G B O D A Z O I C O X O U C
G M R M A N E F R U I M T A N E D L L E F U O N G H K E A S A
N A I A C T T O D R I B B K N R A T S T U R I C E Y O A T O P
H N O S T O R A K O L S W E R Y U S F E M U R U T R C S I N G
O Y T H E L D I H O S A A K O X L A H Q I S N R G H N E E K J
H C T Y L O S A U R U S U A D S T R U L T R C H I I V O S A U
R U S V E G L O M I R R A N T O A L L R O I T E O N E R A T O
V P S T H I E T E T A Q N S B R L U K U S A U T I O I C S U N
J K E J S S Y A R C E S V A R N K R R W A R R A S S E L L I M
I T E I S T M O U A U R E S A S A S A U I S G D M A J U D N A
A B Y R E O T A S A U S R R N A N T O D S I M E B U C H U W X
C S E N E O T D E R N P T N T Q E W S B R U E C L R V E N T I
Z D A N G E R E G O G E S A R E R O U N I O Y O A U K Y L O L
I A U G E O L O G I C T I M E O S L A L U R U V S S T A P H L
H A P T O S U M H C O E L O P H Y S I S U S N C I U D A D C A
K E N T R O S A U R U S M P T H O S A E U F R U T S L A R M B
D I O S A U U O U U S V C E N T R R O R S A U R U S D R I B S
N O O S A P A T O S A U R U S H D A L R U S W P A L E T O A R
```

Find the following dinosaur names and other terms in the puzzle above.

Apatosaurus	Skeleton	*Archaeopteryx*
Paleontologist	*Coelophysis*	Geologic Time
Edmontosaurus	Skull	*Lambeosaurus*
Ilium	*Kentrosaurus*	Pubis
Pachyrhinosaurus	Ischium	*Plateosaurus*
Vertebrae	*Polacanthus*	Femur
Spinosaurus	Humerus	*Tarbosaurus*
Maxilla	*Troodon*	Paleontology
Tylosaurus	Ribs	*Riojasaurus*

A member of the pachycephalosaur family, *Stegoceras* ("Horny Roof") was smaller than other pachycephalosaurs. It had a thick skull and paleontologists know that the bone thickened as the animal aged; it was also thicker in males than in females. *Stegoceras* lived in North America during the Late Cretaceous.

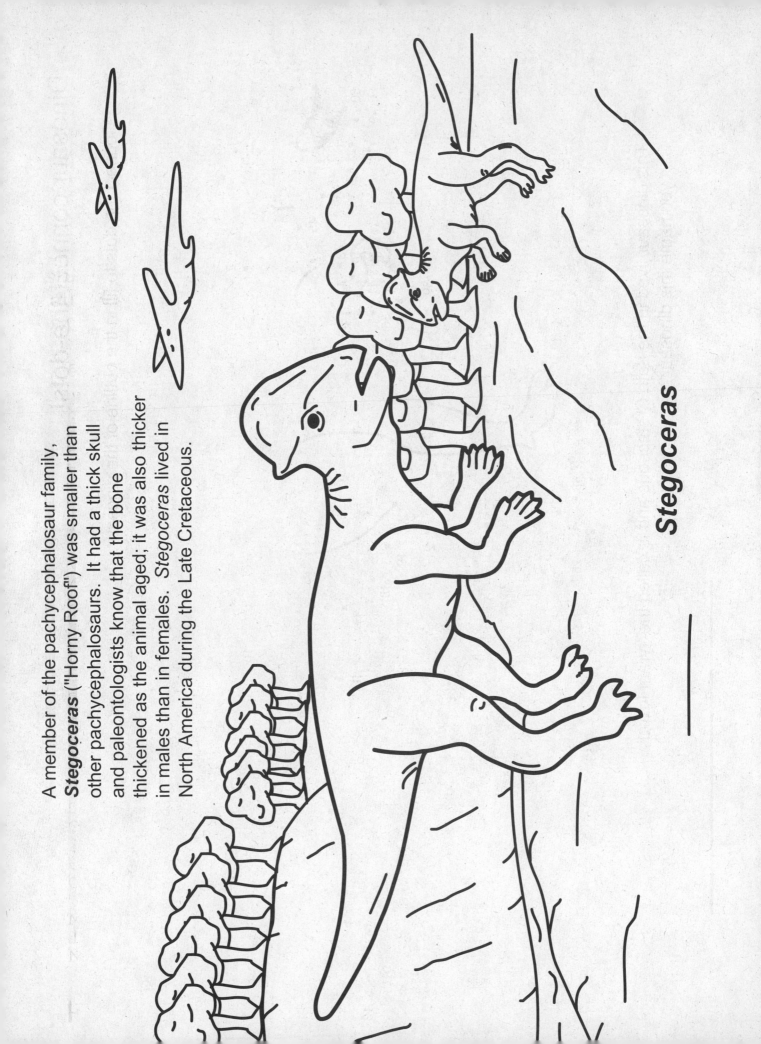

Stegoceras

Dinosaur connect-the-dots!

Connect the dots to fill in the outline of the dinosaur.

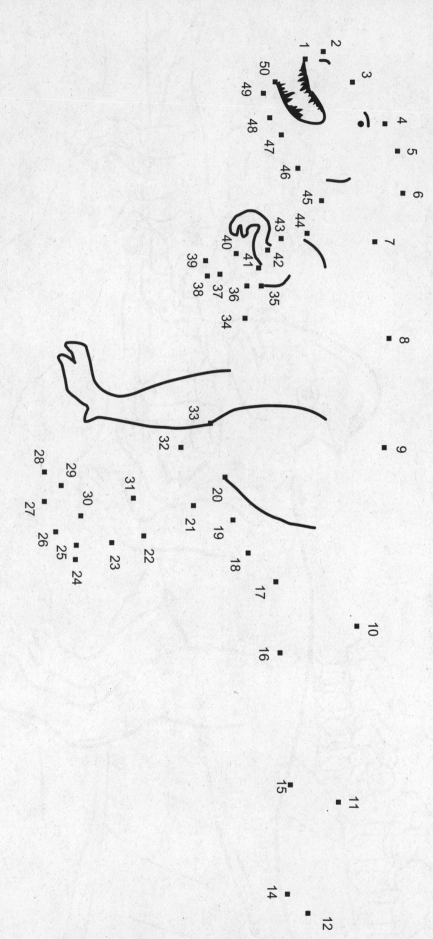

This dinosaur lived in the Late Cretaceous and is called the 'tyrant lizard'.
Can you name this dinosaur?

_____

One of the most distinctive ceratopsians, *Styracosaurus* ("Spiked Lizard") had long bony spikes growing on the neck frill to protect its neck and body and a single, long nasal horn. *Styracosaurus* was an herbivore and lived in North America during the Late Cretaceous.

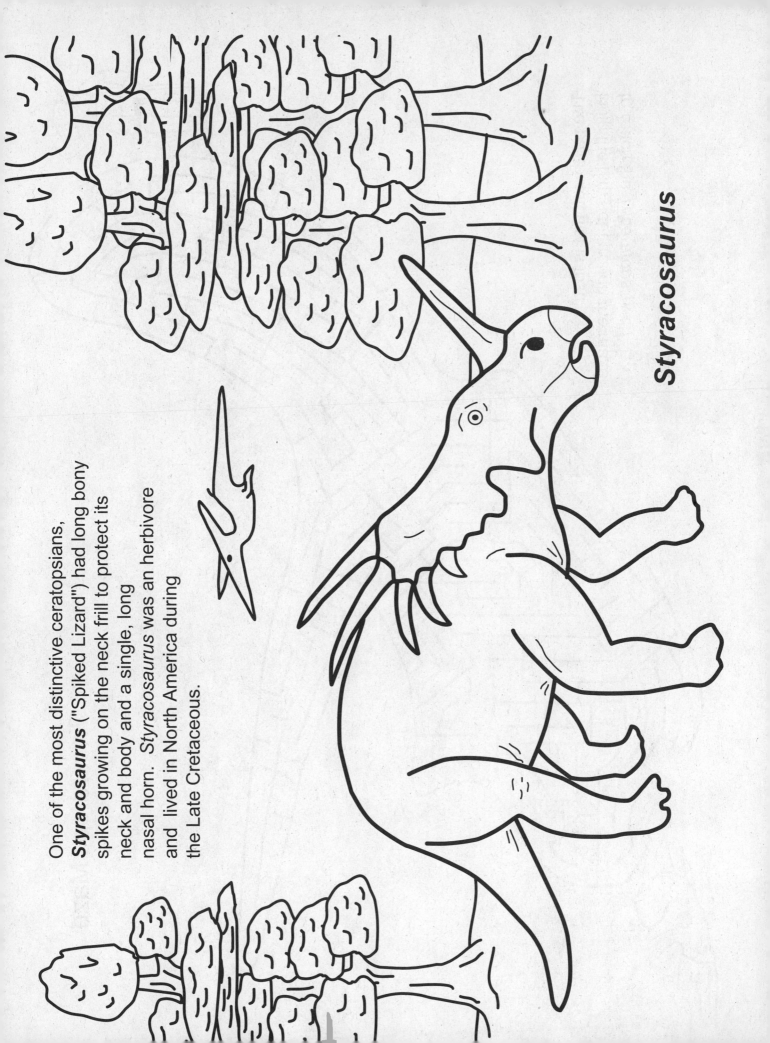

Styracosaurus

The paleontologist is lost!
Help the him get through the maze
to reach the *Triceratops* skull.

Triceratops Maze

Tyrannosaurus
Skull

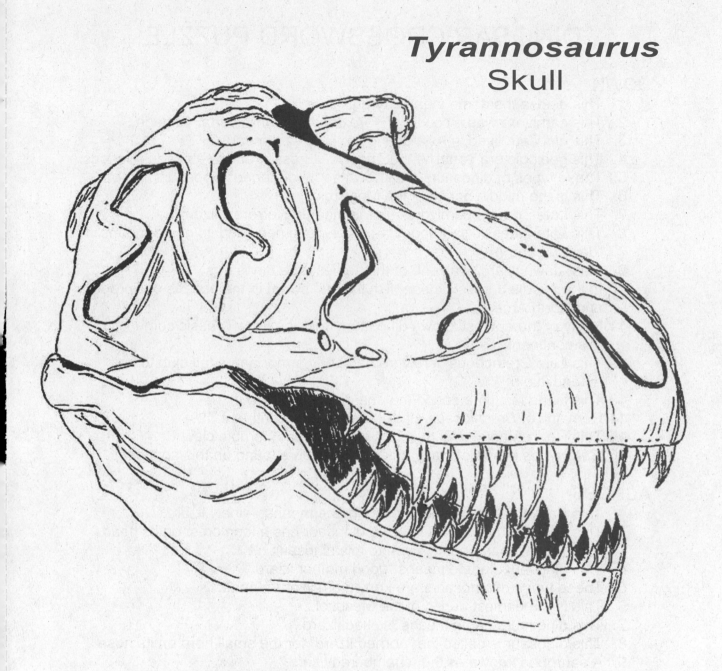

The massive skull of *Tyrannosaurus*
was designed to crush bone and tear flesh.

The skulls of adult *Tyrannosaurs* were 5 to 6 feet in
length and its teeth were 6 to 8 inch long daggers.

Despite its large size, the tyrannosaur brain was
very small. Its one advantage were its large olfactory
lobes, these gave *Tyrannosaurus* a great
sense of smell!

DINOSAR CROSSWORD PUZZLE

DOWN

1. This dinosaur's name means "tyrant lizard."
2. This carnivore was a cousin of *T. rex* and lived in Alberta, Canada.
3. This dinosaur lived in Asia during the Late Cretaceous.
4. This geologic era contains the Triassic, Jurassic, and Cretaceous periods.
5. These types of dinosaurs are known as "bird-hipped" dinosaurs.
6. This is the middle period of the Mesozoic.
7. This Late Triassic carnivore's name means "Herrera's lizard."
8. This Late Jurassic sauropod had a very long neck and its name means "double beam".
9. This "dawn lizard" was one of the earliest true dinosaurs.
10. In the Middle Jurassic these "fish lizards" swam in the oceans of Europe and North America.
11. Many of the earliest known dinosaurs from the Late Triassic come from this continent.
12. This Late Cretaceous herbivore had body armor and a tail club to help defend itself.
13. This is the last time period that the dinosaurs lived in.
14. Remains of *Brachiosaurus* are found on this continent.
15. This North American carnivore's name means "terrible claw."
16. *Gallimimus* is one of many types of dinosaurs found on this continent.

ACROSS

1. This Early Cretaceous herbivore's name means, "sinew lizard."
2. This Late Cretaceous duck-billed dinosaur has a long crest on its head.
3. "Horny roof" is the name given to this dinosaur.
4. This dinosaur's name means "good mother lizard."
5. These types of dinosaurs are known as "lizard-hipped."
6. This is the earliest period of the Mesozoic.
7. This dinosaurs name means "spiked lizard."
8. This dinosaur is called the "horned lizard" for the small horn on its nose.
9. A sauropod known as the "chambered lizard."
10. This Cretaceous dinosaur's name means "Iguana tooth."
11. This "roofed lizard" has spikes on its tail to defend itself.
12. One type of aquatic reptile from the Late Jurassic of Europe.
13. This dinosaur grew up to 30 feet long and lived in South America in the Late Triassic.
14. Late Jurassic carnivore from North America, Africa, and Australia.
15. The first dinosaur to be named, *Iguanodon*, was found on this continent.
16. A flying reptile whose name means, "wing tooth."
17. Probably the most popular of the horned dinosaurs, this dinosaur's name means "three horned face."
18. One of the largest sauropods, this dinosaur is known as the "arm lizard."

Dinosaur
Crossword
Puzzle

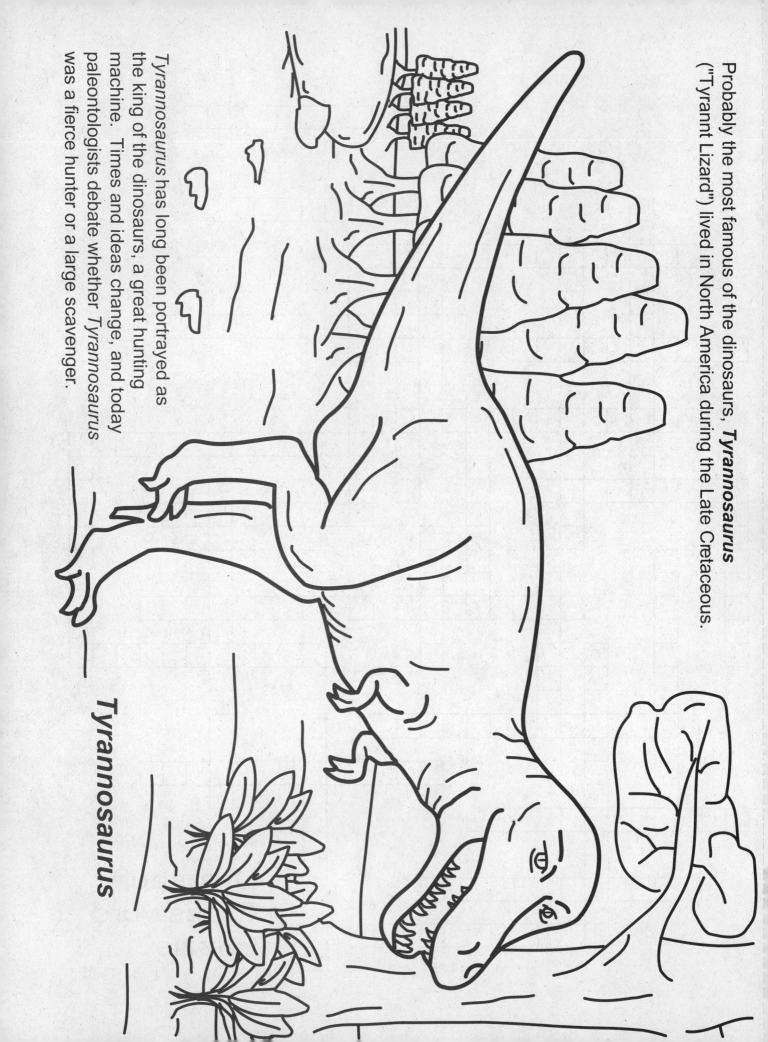

Probably the most famous of the dinosaurs, *Tyrannosaurus* ("Tyrant Lizard") lived in North America during the Late Cretaceous.

Tyrannosaurus has long been portrayed as the king of the dinosaurs, a great hunting machine. Times and ideas change, and today paleontologists debate whether *Tyrannosaurus* was a fierce hunter or a large scavenger.

Tyrannosaurus

Dinosaur Extinction, Part 1

At the end of the Cretaceous, all of the non-avian dinosaurs (all the dinosaurs except for birds) and many other animals on land and in the sea went extinct.

What is an extinction?
An extinction is when all of the animals from one species die out.

What happened at the end of the Cretaceous is called a **mass extinction**, and is known as the K/T Extinction.

A mass extinction is an event that happens all over the planet in a geologically short period of time, sometimes 10 million years or less.

During the K/T Extinction, half of the genera of all the animals on Earth went extinct.

But what caused the extinction of the dinosaurs? There are many theories, and paleontologists still debate what may have happened.

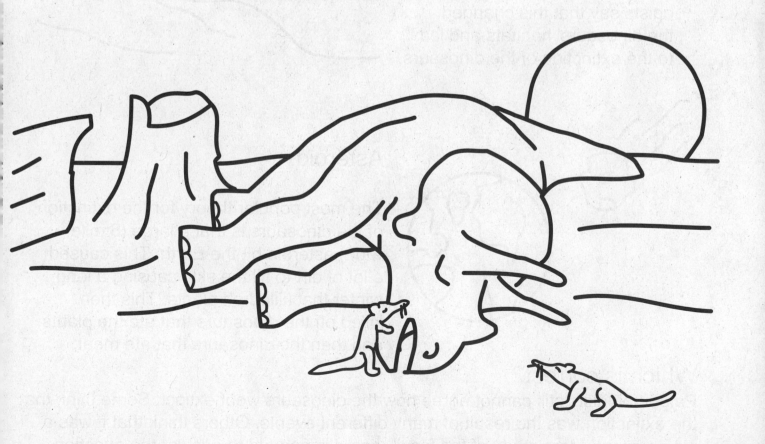

Dinosaur Extinction, Part 2

There are three major ways that paleontologists think could have been the cause of the K/T Extinction event.

Volcanoes:

Some paleontologists say an increase in volcanic eruptions at the end of the Cretaceous is the cause for the extinction of the dinosaurs.

Falling Sea Level:

During the Cretaceous the sea level fell very quickly. Paleontologists say that this changed the dinosaurs' habitats and led to the extinction of the dinosaurs.

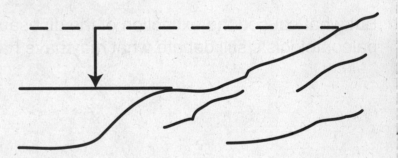

Asteroid:

The most popular theory for the extinction of the dinosaurs is that a large (6 mile wide) asteroid hit the Earth. This caused a lot of dirt to fill the sky, causing a long winter that killed off plants. This then killed off the dinosaurs that ate the plants, and then the dinosaurs that ate meat.

Which is correct?

Paleontologists still cannot agree how the dinosaurs went extinct. Some think that the extinction was the result of many different events. Others think that it was a single event. More study of the fossil record is needed to answer the question.

Stegosaurus skeleton

The non-bird dinosaurs went extinct 65 million years ago, but they still live on in our imagination. Giants like *Tyrannosaurus*, *Triceratops*, *Diplodocus*, and others can now only be brought to life by paleontologists, scientists, and artists. Paleontologists continue to search for dinosaur fossils and we will be able to see the results of their work in museums around the world.

A glossary of animals found in this book:

Albertosaurus (al-BERT-oh-SORE-rus: "Alberta lizard"): Family: Tyrannosauridae. A dinosaur that lived in North America during the Late Cretaceous (78-65 MA). Carnivore.

Allosaurus (al-oh-SORE-us: "other lizard"): Family: Allosauridae. A dinosaur that lived in North America during the Late Jurassic (156-130 MA). Carnivore.

Apatosaurus (ah-PAT-oh-SORE-us: "deceptive reptile"): Family: Diplodocidae. A dinosaur that lived in North America during the Late Jurassic (156-150 MA). Herbivore.

Archaeopteryx (ark-ee-OP-ter-iks "ancient wing"): Family: Achaeopterygidae. A bird that lived in Europe during the Late Jurassic (156-150 MA). Carnivore.

Bothriolepis (ba-th-rio-LEP-is): Family: Bothriolepidae. An armored fish that lived in North America during the Late Devonian (374-360 MA).

Brachiosaurus (brak-ee-oh-SORE-us "arm lizard"): Family: Brachiosauridae. A dinosaur that lived in Africa and North America during the Late Jurassic (153-146 MA). Herbivore.

Camarasaurus (kam-are-ah-SORE-us "chambered lizard"): Family: Camarasauridae. A dinosaur that lived in North America during the Late Jurassic. (155-150 MA). Herbivore.

Ceratosaurus (she-rat-oh-SORE-us "horned lizard"): Family: Ceratosauria. A dinosaur that lived in North America during the Late Jurassic (150 MA). Carnivore.

Coelophysis (SEEL-oh-FIE-sis "hollow form"): Family: Coelophysidae. A dinosaur that lived in North America during the Triassic (225-205 MA). Carnivore.

Cryptoclidus (krip-toh-KLY-dus): Family: Cryptoclididae. A marine reptile that lived during the Late Jurassic (163-144 MA). Carnivore.

Cryptolithus (krip-toh-LITH-us): Phylum: Arthropoda. Order: Polymerida. A trilobite that lived in North America during the Middle Ordovician (471-460 MA).

Deinonychus (die-NON-i-kus "terrible claw"): Family: Dromaeosauridae. A dinosaur that lived in North America during the Early Cretaceous (115-105 MA). Carnivore.

Diplodocus (di-PLOH-de-kus "double beam"): Family: Diplodocidae. A dinosaur that lived in North America during the Late Jurassic (155-146 MA). Herbivore.

Edaphosaurus (ee-daff-oh-SORE-us): Family: Edaphosauridae. A synapsid that lived during the Late Pennsylvanian and Early Permian (300-270 MA). Herbivore.

Edmontosaurus (ed-MON-toh-SORE-us "Edmonton lizard"): Family: Hadrosauridae. A dinosaur that lived in North America during the Late Cretaceous (67-65 MA). Herbivore.

Eoraptor (EE-oh-RAP-tor "dawn hunter"): A dinosaur that lived in South America during the Late Triassic (228-217 MA). Carnivore.

Euoplocephalus (you-op-loh-SEF-ah-lus "true plated head"): Family: Ankylosauridae. A dinosaur that lived in North America during the Late Cretaceous (73-68 MA). Herbivore.

Gallimimus (gal-lee-MEEM-us "chicken mimic"): Family: Ornithomimidae. A dinosaur that lived in Asia during the Late Cretaceous (70-68 MA). Carnivore.

Herrerasaurus (eh-ray-rah-SORE-us "Herrera's lizard"): Family: Herrerasauridae. A dinosaur that lived in South America during the Late Triassic (228-217 MA). Carnivore.

Ichthyosaurus (ik-the-oh-SORE-us "fish lizard"): Family: Ichthyosauridae. A marine reptile that lived in Europe during the Late Jurassic (163-144 MA). Carnivore.

Iguanodon (ig-WHA-noh-don "iguana tooth"): Family: Iguanodontidae. A dinosaur that lived in Europe during the Early Cretaceous (140-110 MA). Herbivore.

Kentrosaurus (KEN-troh-SORE-us "spiky lizard"): Family: Stegosauridae. A dinosaur that lived in Africa during the Late Jurassic (156-150 MA). Herbivore.

Lambeosaurus (LAM-bee-oh-SORE-us "Lambe's lizard"): Family: Hadrosauridae. A duck-billed dinosaur that lived in North America during the Late Cretaceous (75-70 MA). Herbivore.

Maiasaura (MY-ah-SORE-ah "good mother lizard"): Family: Hadrosauridae. A dinosaur that lived in North America during the Late Cretaceous (80-75 MA). Herbivore.

Megazostrodon (may-gah-ZOOS-tro-don): Class: Mammalia, Order: Triconodonta. An early mammal that lived during the Early Jurassic (200-180 MA) Omnivore.

Pachyrhinosaurus (PAK-ee-RINE-oh-SORE-us "thick-nosed reptile"): Family: Ceratopsidae. A dinosaur that lived in North America during the Late Cretaceous (70-65 MA). Herbivore.

Parasaurolophus (par-a-SORE-oh-LOAF-us "beside *Saurolophus*"): Family: Hadrosauridae. A dinosaur that lived in North America during the Late Cretaceous (80-75 MA). Herbivore.

Plateosaurus (PLAT-ee-oh-SORE-us "flat lizard"): Family: Plateosauridae. An early dinosaur that lived in Europe during the Early Triassic (210-203 MA). Herbivore.

Polacanthus (pol-a-KAN-thus "many spines"): Family: Ankylosauridae. An armored dinosaur that lived in Europe during the Early Cretaceous (130-125 MA). Herbivore.

Pteranodon (TER-an-oh-don "wing tooth"): Family: Pterodactyloidae. A reptile that lived in North America during the Cretaceous (113-73 MA). Carnivore.

Riojasaurus (ree-O-ha-SORE-us "La Rioja lizard"): Family: Melanorosauridae. A dinosaur that lived in South America during the Late Triassic (217-204 MA). Herbivore.

Spinosaurus (SPINE-oh-SORE-us "thorn lizard"): Family: Spinosauridae. A dinosaur that lived in Africa during the Late Cretaceous (100-94 MA). Carnivore.

Stegoceras (ste-GOS-er-as "horny roof"): Family: Pachycephalosauridae. A dinosaur that lived in North America during the Late Cretaceous (68-65 MA). Herbivore.

Stegosaurus (STEG-oh-SORE-us "roofed lizard"): Family: Stegosauridae. A dinosaur that lived in North America during the Late Jurassic (156-146 MA). Herbivore.

Styracosaurus (sty-RAK-oh-SORE-us "spiked lizard"): Family: Ceratopsidae. A dinosaur that lived in North America during the Late Cretaceous (75-72 MA). Herbivore.

Tarbosaurus (TAR-boh-SORE-us "alarming lizard"): Family: Tyrannosauridae. A dinosaur that lived in Asia during the Late Cretaceous (84-68 MA). Carnivore.

Tenontosaurus (TEH-NON-toh-SORE-us "sinew lizard"): Family: Hypsilophodontidae. A dinosaur that lived in North America during the Cretaceous (113-108 MA). Herbivore.

Triceratops (try-SERRA-tops "three-horned face"): Family: Ceratopsidae. A dinosaur that lived in North America during the Late Cretaceous (67-65 MA). Herbivore.

Troodon (TROH-oh-don "wounding tooth"): Family: Troodontidae. A dinosaur that lived in North America during the Late Cretaceous (75-65 MA). Carnivore.

Tylosaurus (tie-lo-SORE-us): Family: Mosasauridae. A marine reptile that lived in North America during the Late Cretaceous (97.5-65 MA). Carnivore.

Tyrannosaurus (tie-RAN-oh-SORE-us "tyrant lizard"): Family: Tyrannosauridae. A dinosaur that lived in North America during the Late Cretaceous (72-65 MA). Carnivore.

DINOSAUR WORD SEARCH SOLUTIONS

```
D B F H J L N B A C E G I A K M O Q S U W Y B S I E V J T D C
Q T L E V E O R A P T O R R T N H O N B A P O T S V U R U S T
C F I L E A R A P T O R O R E U E X A D G A J E M O R U N Q W
N P R S S R I C H T H Y O S A U R R U S O R M G E N P S V Y L
E V D B G I C H T H I O S A U R R U S C P A T O Z I C L N G D
U W Y A C E G I K M O Q S U H W E H K M Q S T S M Q K H S L P
S T I G U A N O D O N A E S A U R U S D L A I A S P N D O N Y
R A C A E D L S Q N I A T L C A M A R A S A U R U S P Z H J D
L O L L I N E A P Z I C F G H O S N A P E R I R G S J D I K S
L P N L G O E U O P L O C E P H A L U S C O A U T E D I V P I
A J L I B E R R T O S E A U R I U U S A L L S S A U P U K U
S U A M U R I U S C H R I A W N R S O U U O T A M L E L R D C
O R N I T H I S C H I A N T L A U N G R O P O M E S O Z O I C
G A R M A P E F R U I T T A R N S D L I E H M O A R D D E P R
N S I U C E T O D R I O N K N E A T O S T U R I C E R O A L O
H S O S T Y R A C O S A U R U S W O D C A S B O U T U C S O N
O I T H E R D I N O S A A U R S H I A H T I T N P G R U E D K
H C R Y P T O C L E I D U S A D E T R I C E R A T O P S O O U
R U S V E E L O C I R R A P T O R Y P A R O I T E O C E R C T
M P S T H N E T Y T A U N A T Y R A N N O S A U R U S I C U U
A K A L L O S A U R U S S T R N E R L D W A S R A S B E L S I
I S E I S N M O S A U R U S P A R A S A B I S G N A N I M D N
A L B E R T O S A U R U S R N A A N T O D E I N O N Y C H U S
S S E N E O T D O R N P R N T Q S W Y S I R C E D L A V E N T
A D A N G S T E G O C E R A S E A L O U N S L Y O A N K Y L O
U A U G R A U S O F U R A S N O U E L A O U R U N S U T A P H
R A P T O U R M H O N O D C L O R F N I S U S N C I U D A D C
A R L Y C R E T A C E O U S T H U S A U A F R U T S L A R M
S I O S A U U O R U S V C E N T S L R O U S A U R U S D T I T
N O O S A S U R U I S C E N P I H D C E R A T O S A U R U S A
```

Which is the dinosaur? (Answers)

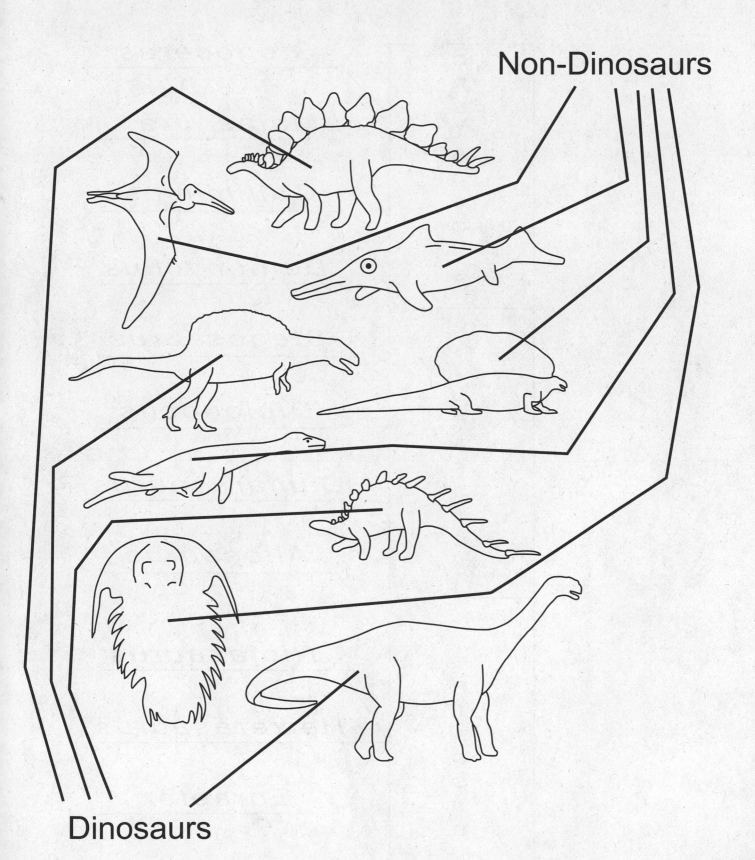

Non-Dinosaurs

Dinosaurs

Time Scale Matching Answers

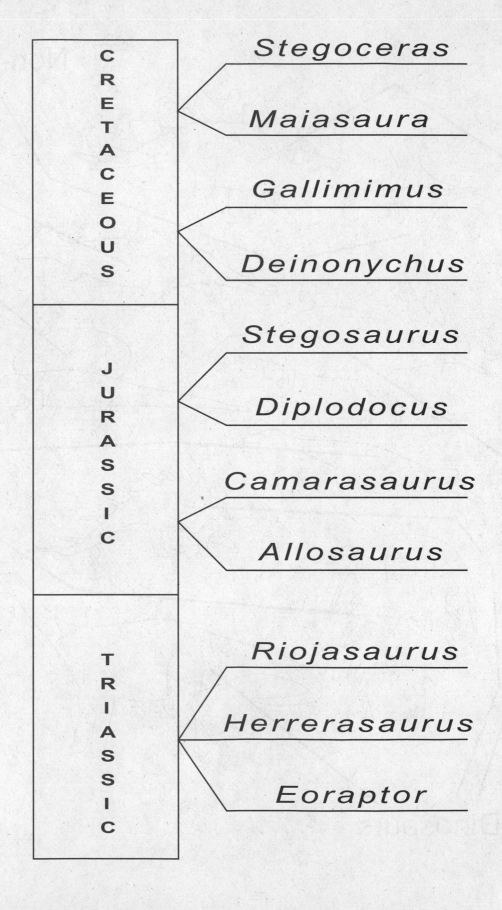

CRETACEOUS

Stegoceras

Maiasaura

Gallimimus

Deinonychus

JURASSIC

Stegosaurus

Diplodocus

Camarasaurus

Allosaurus

TRIASSIC

Riojasaurus

Herrerasaurus

Eoraptor

Dinosaur Dentistry!
Answers

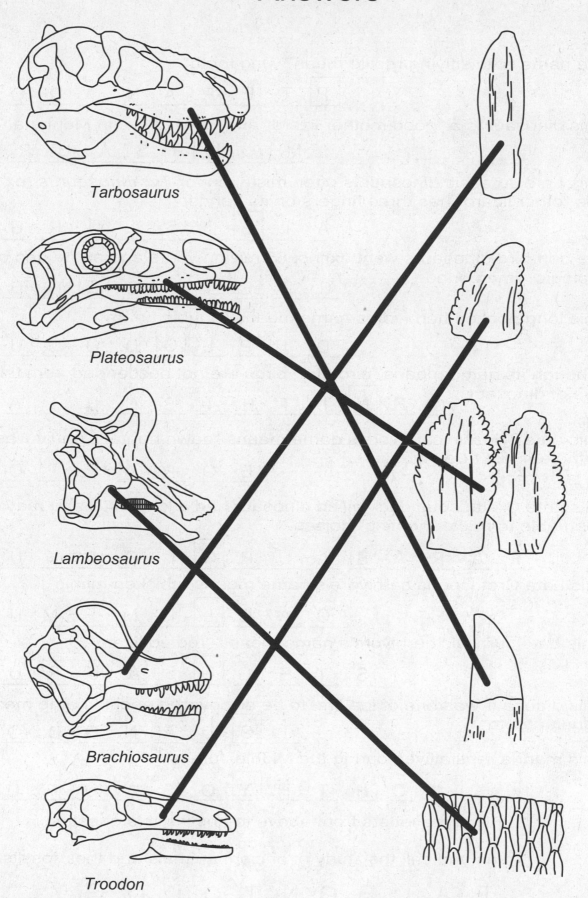

Tarbosaurus

Plateosaurus

Lambeosaurus

Brachiosaurus

Troodon

DINOSAUR DEFINITIONS

The name of this flying reptile mean "wing tooth".

P T E R A N O D O N

This dinosaur is a "good mother lizard" and used to live in Montana.

M A I A S A U R A

This Late Jurassic dinosaur is often mistaken for *Tyrannosaurus rex* but this "other lizard" has three fingers on its hands.

A L L O S A U R U S

The non-bird dinosaurs went extinct 65 million years ago at the end of this geologic time period.

C R E T A C E O U S

This long necked herbivores name means "double beam".

D I P L O D O C U S

Although its name means "bird hip", birds are not descended from this type of dinosaur.

O R N I T H I S C H I A N

This Late Triassic carnivore's name means "dawn hunter", and it was one of the earliest true dinosaurs.

E O R A P T O R

This Late Cretaceous duck-billed dinosaur had a long skull and may have been able to make "hooting" noises.

P A R A S A U R O L O P H U S

This Late Cretaceous carnivore's name means "chicken mimic".

G A L L I M I M U S

This Late Jurassic herbivore's name means "roofed lizard".

S T E G O S A U R U S

This dinosaur was one of the first to be discovered and its name means "iguana tooth".

I G U A N O D O N

This marine reptile lived during the Middle Jurassic.

I C H T H Y O S A U R U S

Fill in the letters from above to answer this question.

What do you call the study of ancient animals and their fossils?

P A L E O N T O L O G Y

Dinosaur skeleton matching.
(Answers)

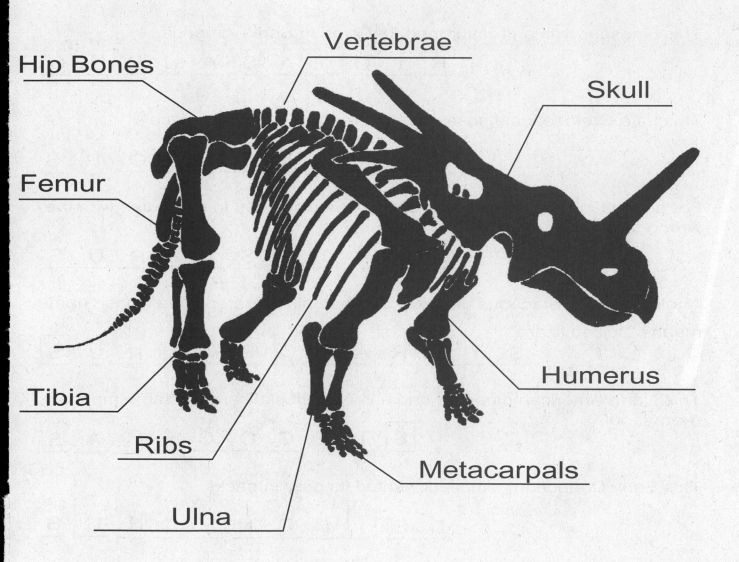

Hip Bones

Vertebrae

Skull

Femur

Tibia

Ribs

Ulna

Metacarpals

Humerus

DINOSAUR DEFINITIONS TWO

This "tyrant lizard" lived during the Late Cretaceous.

T Y R A N N O S A U R U S

This dinosaur was a prosauropod that lived in South America.

R I O J A S A U R U S

This Late Cretaceous dinosaurs name means "three horn face".

T R I C E R A T O P S

For a long time this "deceptive reptile" was displayed in museums with the wrong skull on its skeleton.

A P A T O S A U R U S

Another Late Cretaceous dinosaur of the family Ceratopsidae whose name means "spiked lizard".

S T Y R A C O S A U R U S

This North American dinosaur had a very thick skull and its name means "horny roof".

S T E G O C E R A S

This Early Cretaceous dinosaur hunted its prey in packs.

D E I N O N Y C H U S

One of the earliest dinosaurs, this dinosaur's name means "hollow form".

C O E L O P H Y S I S

Fill in the letters from above to answer this question.
In which geologic time period did the first dinosaurs live?

T R I A S S I C

SECOND DINOSAUR WORD SEARCH SOLUTIONS

```
D PUBIS NDACEKIKMO P SLLABJ SKELETON
QTLEPNDOEFIEKTN RIOJASAURUS RUSDT
C VERTEBRAE RNORUBXA L GHJIMORUNQ P W
NPRSLRPQNLJTF SPINOSAURUS NPSVY L L
EVDBECAWPW I RJHX A WVCP C TRZICLNGA D
TROODON BKMSQSUW R LKMQ L AXMQKHSLT P
STGODONOSA C SEAU C UE T RA T NIAPDONE Y
RACEEDLHQN H ACAM H RAOLKAUTPZHJNO D
LOLKI P ERPZIUGHO A NAP N WRC G HJLIKS S
MPNVG A JKLQURDMY E TOYC T BUTS U HVPA Z
AGLIB L RRTOMRAURO U SELHOSOS P SUR S
XEANU E IUS L HTIAN P SOTUO S LAM A LR T RA
IR EDMONTOSAURUS TNGBODA Z OIC O Y U C
GMRMA N EFRUI M TANEDLLEF U ONG H KEASA
NAIACT T TODRI B BKNRATSTUR I CEY Y ATOP
HNOST O RAKOLSW E RYUS FEMUR TR C SING
OYTHE L DIHOSAA O XLAHQIS N RG I NEEKJ
HC TYLOSAURUS UAD S TRUL T RCHI I VOSAU
RUSVE G LO M IRRANTO A LLROITEC N ERATO
VPSTHI E TE T AQNSBRL U KUSAUTI O ICSUN
JKEJS S YA R CESVARN K R WARRA S ELEI M
ITEIS T MO U AURESA S ASAU I SGD M AJUDNA
ABYREOTA S AUSRRNANTOD S IMEBUCHUW X
CSENEOTDERNPTNTQEWSBRU C LRVENTI L
ZDANGEREGOGESAREROUN I OYOAUKYLO L
IAU GEOLOGICTIME OSLALURUVSTAPHL A
HAPTOSUMH COELOPHYSIS USNCIUDADC A
KENTROSAURUS MPTHOSAEUFRUTSLARM B
DIOSAUUOUSVCENTRRORSAURUSD RIBS
NOOS APATOSAURUS HDALRUSWPALETOAR
```

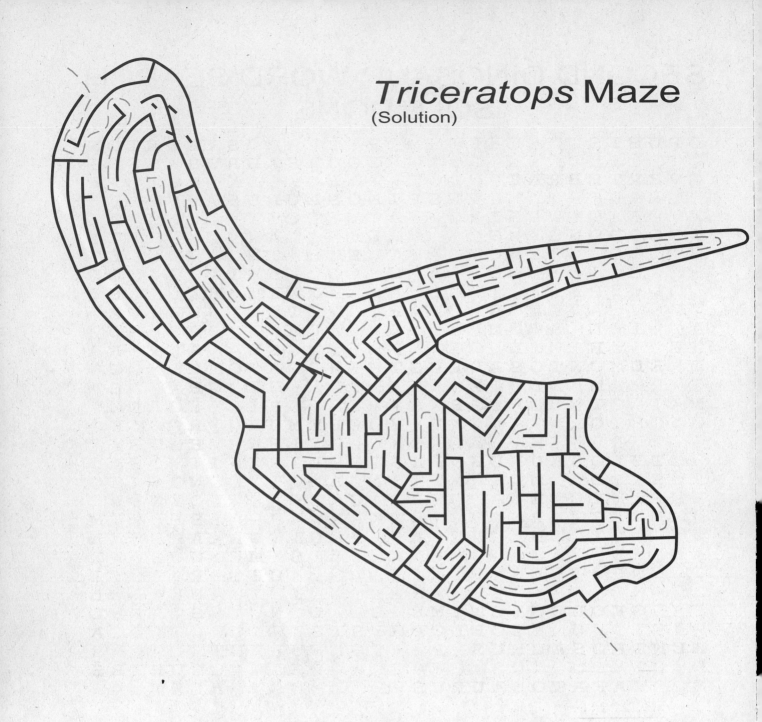

Triceratops Maze
(Solution)

Dinosaur Crossword Puzzle

(Solutions)